THE PERSIAN HERO GUSHTAP KILLING THE DRAGON.

From a Persian edition of Firdausi's poem, *Shah Namah*, seventeenth century. Cochran Collection, Metropolitan Museum.

DRAGONS
AND
DRAGON LORE

ERNEST INGERSOLL

INTRODUCTION BY
HENRY FAIRFIELD OSBORN

DOVER PUBLICATIONS, INC.
MINEOLA, NEW YORK

Bibliographical Note

This Dover edition, first published in 2005, is an unabridged republication of the edition published by Payson & Clarke Ltd., New York, 1928.

Library of Congress Cataloging-in-Publication Data

Ingersoll, Ernest, 1852–1946.
    Dragons and dragon lore / Ernest Ingersoll ; with an introduction by Henry Fairfield Osborn.
        p. cm.
    Originally published: New York : Payson & Clarke, 1928.
    Includes bibliographical references and index.
    ISBN 0-486-44074-5 (pbk.)
    1. Dragons. 2. Animals, Mythical. 3. Animals—Folklore. I. Title.

GR830.D715 2005
398'.469—dc22
                                                        2004061898

Manufactured in the United States of America
Dover Publications, Inc., 31 East 2nd Street, Mineola, N.Y. 11501

INTRODUCTION

I became intensely interested in Dragon Worship and the Dragon Myth during my recent journey in China and Mongolia in support of the Central Asiatic Expeditions of Roy Chapman Andrews. Especially, in the royal city of Peking appears the apotheosis of the Dragon in every conceivable form of symbolism and architecture. The Dragons leading up to the steps of the temples and palaces of the Manchu emperors, and the superb dragon-screen guarding the approach to one of the royal palaces, are but two of the innumerable examples of the universal former belief in these mythical animals, and of the still prevailing beliefs among the common people of China.

For example, one night in a far distant telegraph station in the heart of the desert of Gobi, I overheard two men pointing out Leader Andrews and myself as 'men of the Dragon bones.' On inquiry, I learned that our great Central Asiatic Expedition was universally regarded by the natives as engaged in the quest of remains of extinct Dragons, and that this superstition is connected with the still universal belief among the natives that fossil bones, and especially fossil teeth have a high medicinal value.

Not long after my return from Central Asia, I suggested to my friend, Ernest Ingersoll, that he write the present volume, preparing a fresh study of the history of the Dragon Myth which, now largely confined to China, once spread all over Asia and Europe, as dominant not only in mythology but entering even into the early teachings of Christianity, as so many other pagan myths have done. I knew that the author was well-qualified for a work of this character, because of his remarkable success in previous volumes for old and young, and in his original observations on various forms of animal life, from the American oyster to many birds and mammals. He is especially versed, perhaps, in regard to one very interesting question which is often asked, namely, how far the animals of myth and of legend, like the Dragon, the Hydra, the Phœnix, the Unicorn and the Mermaid, are products of pure imagination, and how far due to some fancied resemblance of a living form or to the tales of travelers. For example, it occurred to me, while examining the giant fossil eggs of the extinct ostrich of China (now known under the scientific name *Struthiolithus,* assigned by the late Doctor Eastman), that it may have given rise to the myth of the Phœnix or of the Roc. On this point, the author sends me the following very interesting notes:

I have not studied the Unicorn. . . . The Mermaid is usually attributed to somebody's story of seeing a dugong nursing its baby, but I guess the idea goes back to the time when old Poseidon was half man, half fish, and had plenty of watermaidens, half woman, half fish, disporting around him. The first time anyone saw Mistress Venus she was in that 'semi' shape if I remember rightly. . . . I do not find the Roc indigenous in the Far East, and I greatly doubt whether anywhere it had a 'physical' progenitor, or was suggested by any big, extinct, ratite egg. I have discussed this in my "Birds in Legend, Fable and Folklore," and conclude it to be a figment of an ancient boasting storyteller's fancy. . . . The only other

vi

imaginary form of importance *in China is the* Feng—*a pheasant-like 'bird' analogous to the Phœnix—and probably hatched in the same sun-nest.* . . . *As to your query about 'mythical' and 'legendary' animals: My whole thesis in regard to the Dragon is that it is entirely imaginary; and I regard the Hydra (absent from the Chinese mind) as merely an extravagance that arose in the West, perhaps by confusion of snake and octopus.*

I feel confident that the present work will arouse a widespread interest among students of animal form and history on the one hand, and of folk-lore, primitive religion and mythology on the other.

HENRY FAIRFIELD OSBORN.

American Museum of Natural History,
December 20, 1927.

Contents

Illustrations

ILLUSTRATIONS

deeply forked tongue, the lower jaw has no teeth, but the upper is armed with many formidable tusks and cobra-like fangs, and the head bristles with horns and ridges amid which an eye like that of a serpent glares balefully. This is the best representation of the head of the dragon, according to modern standards, that is available to me, and I offer sincere thanks to the American Museum of Natural History for placing its unrivalled facilities for photographing difficult subjects, and enabling its operator, Mr. H. S. Rice, to execute for me this beautiful illustration. The candlestick is in my possession and is shown by courtesy of Mrs. Frances Buchanan Ingersoll.

A Japanese lacquered table-pedestal supported by entwined serpentine dragons, and a bronze sword guard with dragons amid clouds, signed 'Icheriu Tomoyoshi, 1829.' Note the grasped 'pearl.' Courtesy of the Metropolitan Museum.

These French stone sculptures of the fourteenth and fifteenth centuries are in the Metropolitan Museum Cloisters. The image of the dragon stands about three and a half feet high, and appears much weathered. Note its goat-like ears and beard, and bat's wings. The obscure markings on the wings are well cut human eyes, two in each section of both wings; the feet are bird-like, the scales and tail ophidian. The statue of St. Michael is about two feet tall.

The illustration shows the upper half of a painted altar-piece, in the British Royal Collection, supposed to be by a Dutch artist in the fifteenth century. King Henry VII and his family are encamped in the foreground, here indicated only by the tents and faces. Rothery reproduces the whole painting in his 'Armorial Bearings of the Princes of Wales.'

The central figure is a highly conventionalized, ninth century illustration of a Celtic dragon. The heraldic silhouettes represent (left) a supporter on the arms of Henry VIII of England (right), the same on Queen Elizabeth's arms. A similar (red) dragon is now a part of the achievement of a Prince of Wales. From Rothery.

Engraved by Louis Surugne from the painting.

The archangel slaying the leader of the revolt in heaven, an Italian carving of the fifteenth century. The figure of St. George (right) is a German wooden statuette dated about 1480. Courtesy of the Metropolitan Museum.

ILLUSTRATIONS

DRAGONS AND DRAGON LORE

Chapter One

BIRTH OF THE DRAGON

TODAY a solar eclipse is slowly darkening my study window, and when I step out of doors to watch it I hear a man say: The Dragon is eating the sun.

No dragon exists—none ever did exist. Nevertheless a belief in its actuality has prevailed since remote antiquity, and has become a fact of historic, social, and artistic interest. Millions of persons to-day have as firm a faith in its reality as in any fact, or supposed fact, of their intuition or experience. As an element in the ancient Oriental creation-myths it is perhaps the most antique product of human imagination; and it stalks, picturesque and portentous, through mediæval legend.

The dragon was born in the youth of the East, a creature engendered between inward fear and outward peril, was nurtured among prehistoric wanderers, and has survived in the hinterlands of ignorance and superstition because it embodied the underlying principle of all morality—the eternal contrast and contest between Good and Evil, typified by the incessant struggle of man with the forces of nature and with his twofold self. In the East the dragon, like the primitive gods, was by turns deity and demon; carried westward, it fell almost wholly into the latter estate, or was transformed into a purely allegorical figure; and it has its counterpart, if not its descendants, in the religious faith and rites of every known land and all sorts of peoples.

13

The dragon is as old as the sensitiveness and imagination of mankind, and doubtless had assumed a definite shape in some crude, material expression as long ago as when men first began to paint, or to carve in wood and on stone, marks and images that were at least symbols of the supposed realities visible to their mental eyes.

It is needless to repeat that the phenomena of nature must have appeared to primitive man as an immense, contradictory, insolvable mystery, a mixture of light and darkness, sunshine and storm, things helpful to him contending, as if animated, with things harmful, life alternating with death and decay. This is an old story, but it is plain that, in common with the more intelligent animals, man's predominant sensation was fear —fear of his brutish fellows, dread of the jungle and its beasts and ogres, of the desert and its burning drouth, of the wind and the thunderous lightning; most of all terror of the dark, peopled with spirits good and bad. Against the unknown and therefore frightful shapes and noises of the night, the shrieks of the gale, awe of the ocean, the flickering lights and sickening miasma of the bog—all to his half-awakened mind evidence of animate beings above his reach or understanding—man knew of but one defense, which was humble propitiation and never-ceasing payment of ransom. Ghosts blackmailed him throughout his terror-stricken life. The only friendly things in nature were sunshine and water—most of all gentle, nourishing rain: what wonder then that the most beneficent spirits and primary deities in all the primitive cults of Europe and Asia, at least, have been those connected with fresh waters. When one attempts to trace to its birth the creature or concept of which we are in search, one is led backward and backward to the very beginning of human philosophy. That origin seems to rest in the earliest discoverable traces of human thought on this earth, when paleolithic man cowered over woodland campfires or watched by night beside Asiatic rivers, now dry, now mysteriously overflowing, or made magic in some consecrated cave; and when wonder was rising slowly—oh, so slowly—in his brain into the dignity of reasoning. These are really very interesting facts, and they appear to have been true during thousands of bygone years. The strange, half-human figures painted on the wall of a cave in southern France by a Magdalénien artist in the Old Stone Age, and labelled 'Sorcerer' by archæologists, may easily be construed as an attempt to portray an ancestral dragon. Let us try to find the origin of this thing, and to discover not only its meaning, but how or why the Dragon came to be of its present form. It is doubtless a long and complicated story, but there is no call to apologize for either its length or its absurdities.

We have seen that the notion embodied in the word 'dragon' goes back to the beginning of recorded human thoughts about the mysteries of the thinker and his world. It is connected with the powers and doings of the earliest gods, and like them is vague, changeable and contradictory in its attributes, maintaining from first to last only one definable characteristic—association with and control of water. This points unmistakably to its birth in a land where water is the most important thing in nature to human existence—the essential requisite, indeed, for life and happiness. Such are the conditions in the valleys of the Nile and the Euphrates, precisely the regions in which, first of all, mankind began to establish a settled existence and to lay the foundations of civilization in agriculture. The success of agriculture was made possible by the invention of irrigation, through which man obtained command of the water-supply for his fields, and out-witted, so to say, the eccentricities of the rainfall. In timely showers to the right amount, in living streams and their vernal overflows that leave new soil, the rainfall is a blessing; but in the lightning-darting storm, in excessive floods, it may, and sometimes does, become a curse. Primitive men, unlearned in the natural laws by which we now account for the weather, imagined its varying moods to be the result of supernatural powers struggling somewhere in space, on one side for good conditions, on the other towards destruction and chaos; and they invented wondrous and complex stories to explain it. Every change in the weather was attributed to the gods. When rains were favourable, good gods got the credit; when pro-longed drouth or devastating storms assailed the locality, men told one another that malignant spirits were at work.

Supreme among the earliest known divinities of Egypt was Re (or Ra). Associated with him was a feminine deity, Hathor, the 'great Mother,' or source of all earthly life. At enmity with Re was a formless being, Set. As Re grew aged mankind (created by Hathor) showed signs of rebellion, instigated by Set, and a council of the gods advised that Hathor be sent down to earth to subdue her insurgent progeny. She complied, received the additional epithet 'Sekhet,' acquired the ferocious lioness as her symbol, and went about cutting throats until the land was flooded with blood. Alarmed at the destruction of his subjects, which threatened to be total, Re begged Hathor-Sekhet to desist. She refused, whereupon Re caused to be brewed a red liquor, a draft of which subdued Hathor's mani-acal rage, and so a remnant of mankind was saved. From that bloody time Hathor's reputation fell to that of a malignant spirit, for she, who theretofore had been a beneficent 'giver of life' had shown herself, in the avatar of Sekhet, a demon of destruction. In this skeleton of a legend we have the kernel of Egyptian mythology and religion. Re fades out and Osiris appears, an earthly king deified as a sort of water-god, who becomes more definitely a personification of the Nile in its beneficent aspect. Hathor becomes his consort Isis, and they produce a son Horus whose symbol is a falcon, sometimes accompanied by serpents, and who carries on Re's feud with Set (subsequently murderer of Osiris) under various warrior-methods, such as driving to battle in a chariot drawn by griffins (perpetuated in the Greek *gryphon*)—perhaps the most primitive incarnations of the dragon. Set is a water-devil whose followers take the form of crocodiles and other dangerous creatures of the great river; and later we read of a gigantic snake-like reptile Apop, which apparently was that long-lived old monster Set, and which later was known among the gods of Greek Olympus as Typhon, a snake-headed giant. Apop had a corps of typhonic monsters at his call. A host of fabulous monsters seem to have been derived, with more or less claim to true ancestry, from these prehistoric creatures of the Egyptian imagination.

While this epic or drama of the development of the human intelligence was in progress in Egypt, exhibiting the Celestial triad at the basis of all cosmic mythology, a similar development of legendary history was proceeding in Mesopotamia. "The Egyptian legends cannot be fully appreciated," we are told, "unless they are studied in conjunction with those of Babylonia and Assyria, the mythology of Greece, Persia, India, China Indonesia and America." We do not find in the opening chapters of the history of either Egypt or Mesopotamia the characteristic dragons we shall encounter later; but we do discover there the germ and its *raison d'être* of what later became the conventional forms and properties of the Chinese 'lung,' the hydras and giants of Greek myth, and the hero-stories of mediæval St. George. "Egyptian literature," Professor G. Elliot Smith assures us, "affords a clearer insight into the development of the Great Mother, the Water God and the Warrior Sun God, than we can obtain from any other writings of the origin of this fundamental stratum of deities. And in the three legends: The Destruction of Mankind, The Story of the Winged Disk [symbol of Horus], and The Conflict between Horus and Set, it has preserved the germs of the great Dragon Saga. Babylonian literature has shown us how this raw material was worked up into the definite and familiar story, as well as how the features of a variety of animals were blended to form the composite monster. India and Greece, as well as more distant parts of Africa, Europe and Asia, and even America, have preserved many details that have been lost in the real home of the monster."

Physical conditions were much the same in Mesopotamia as in Egypt. Like the Nile, the Euphrates was a permanent river, flowing from the Armenian mountains through a vast expanse of arid, yet fertile, land to the great marshes (now much reduced) at the head of the Persian Gulf. It rose to full banks, or over them, in early summer, fed by melting snow, and the annual inundations along its course were of the highest benefit and importance to the agriculturists settled at least six or seven thousand years ago in its lower basin. As population and tillage increased, irrigation—popularly believed to have been introduced by the gods—became more and more a necessity, and this need of abundant and well-regulated water influenced the local religion, the features of which we have learned from the

18

engraved seals, inscribed tablets, and other evidences exhumed from the ruins of temples and royal houses.

The primitive theory of world-creation and the theogony of these pre-Babylonians are similar to those of Egypt; and the Sumerians, the earliest known permanent residents in the Euphrates Valley, were perhaps allied racially with the men of the Nile country—certainly there was communication between them long before the date of any records yet obtained. There is evidence, moreover, that the peoples whom we know by the earliest 'civilized' remains thus far discovered were preceded in the valleys of both the Euphrates and the Nile by a population far more primitive, which was displaced—in the case of Sumer, presumably by immigrants from southern Persia; for probably the culture represented by Susa is older than that of the cities of Sumer. Both peoples conceived the earth to be an island floating on an infinite expanse and depth of water which welled up around it as an ocean, often imaged forth as an encircling serpent, on whose horizon rested the dome of the sky. At first "darkness was upon the face of the deep," yet the great primeval gods were even then alive,—indistinct, fickle, anthropomorphic originators and representatives of natural phenomena.

The Babylonian god with which we are most concerned is Ea, who seems to stand in about the same relation to the Sumerian myth of creation as did Osiris to the Egyptian. Among the oldest pictures that have come down to us is one of a creature called Oannos—a human figure whose body, from the middle down, is that of a fish. Perhaps it is meant for Ea, who otherwise is represented as a man wearing a fish-skin, as a fish, or as a composite creature with a fish's body and tail. Ea was a water-god, personifying and governing all the waters

19

on the earth, above or under it, including rivers and irrigation canals; nevertheless, although regarded as primarily a personification of the beneficent, life-giving powers of water (as in producing and sustaining crops), he was also identified with the devastating forces of wind and water, as in storms. As Osiris was confusingly reincarnated in Horus, so the earlier Enlil was absorbed in Ea, and gradually Ea in his son Marduk, when he became a sun-god, the slayer of Tiamat the water-demon. Tiamat, chaos personified (with just such a troop of malignant subordinates as attended Set), came out of the murky primeval ocean on purpose to baulk in their creative plans the well-intentioned gods of the air who gave the land the blessed rains on which the people depended for life and happiness. Tiamat was feminine; and this she-dragon, a counterpart of Hathor, heads a long line of 'demons,' good and bad.

The word 'dragon' as we see it written to-day calls to mind the grotesque, writhing figure of Chinese or Japanese ornament; but in this treatise we must accept the term in a far wider scope, as representing supernatural powers in any sense, yet not invariably hateful. As to the matter of sex, demon-women arose very early to vex the sun-gods of Egypt, but they soon became changed in sex, and dragons have been masculine ever since.

What happened to Tiamat is variously explained. Dr. Hopkins [1] summarizes her history, gathered from the tablets and seals recovered from the ruins of Nippur and elsewhere, thus: *

Chaos bred monsters, and then the divine Heaven and

* The small figure above the line in this paragraph, and those elsewhere, correspond to similarly numbered items in the Bibliography at the end of this book.

Earth, as Anshar and Kishar, ancestors of Anu, Enlil, and Ea, prepared for conflict, to maintain order. . . . The eleven opposing monsters of Chaos are created by Tiamat and headed by Kingu, to whom Tiamat gives the tablets of destiny and whom she makes her consort. The peace-loving gods seem to fear; they send a messenger to Tiamat, "May her liver be pacified, her heart softened" [apparently without effect]. . . . At any rate, we next see Bel-Marduk, at the command of his father, going joyfully into battle after preparing for the conflict by making weapons, bow, lance, club, lightning-bolt, storm-winds and a net wherewith to catch Tiamat. The gods get drunk with joy, anticipating victory and hailing Marduk as already lord of the universe. On Storm (his chariot) he rushes forth, haloed with light, from which Kingu shrinks. Him follow the seven winds. Tiamat, however, fears him not, but when Marduk challenges her, she fights, "raging and shaking with fury," yet all in vain. For Marduk stifles her with a poisonous gas ('evil wind'), and then transfixes her, also taking the tablets from Kingu and netting the other monsters. But Tiamat he cuts in two, making one half of her the sky.

What was Tiamat like in the opinion of the people to whom these fanciful accounts of the work and adventures of the gods in bringing order out of chaos were as 'gospel truth'? The most ancient representation of her is an engraving on a cylinder-seal in the British Museum, which shows a thick-bodied snake, the forward third of its body upreared and bearing two little arm-like appendages, its tongue extended and its head crowned with one goat-like horn. If this portrait is really intended for Tiamat, it shows a queer relationship between this sinister sea-demon and the fish-god Ea, who also appears to

21

have been part antelope (gazelle or goat), as is shown by antique pictures of him as a combination of antelope and fish, whence a 'sea-goat' came to be the vehicle of Marduk.

The tradition of Marduk's titanic battle with Tiamat seems to have been preserved in the famous story in the *Apocrypha* of Bel and the Dragon. In the time of the reign of Nebuchadnezzar at Babylon, after the destruction of Jerusalem and the carrying of Judah into captivity, an unconverted Jew named Daniel had risen, with the cleverness of his race, to be the king's favourite and prime minister; and he was naturally hated by the ecclesiastics of the Court, who were justly incensed that a foreigner who persisted in the worship of Yahweh should be so greatly honoured. Scholars disagree as to whether he is the same Daniel who had similar distinction and troubles according to the Book of Daniel, or another man, or whether either of them ever had an existence—but this does not concern us. Among several circumstances not included in the canonical Bible, but narrated in both the Vulgate and Septuagint versions, the one most pertinent to our theme is that in Babylon a huge dragon was worshipped and fed by the people. Daniel refused to pay it homage, and told the king that if permitted he would kill the monster without using any weapons, and so free the populace from its exactions. His majesty consented, whereupon Daniel made a bolus of indigestible materials, mainly pitch (but some say it was a ball of straw filled with sharpened nails), and threw it into the reptile's maw. It was promptly swallowed, wherefore the monster presently 'burst' and died. (One commentator notes that in Hebrew writing the word for 'pitch' looks much like that for 'tornado,' recalling the 'great wind' by which Marduk put an end to Tiamat.) The ungrateful populace, enraged at this Herculean feat demanded Daniel's death, and the king reluctantly cast him into a den of lions kept as royal executioners, where he stayed a full week unharmed, but likely to starve to death—as also were the lions, inhibited by magic from their prey. On the seventh day another Jew, Habbakuk, was cooking dinner for his harvest-hands on his farm somewhere in the country, when he was lifted up by an angel (as once happened to Ezekiel) and carried to the capital with a quantity of provisions to feed the unfortunate reformer. Daniel was thereupon restored to liberty and power as chief magician, and the famishing lions were fed with humbler priests.

Very ancient Babylonian drawings show Tiamat harnessed to a four-wheeled chariot in which is seated a god who, in the opinion of Dr. William Hayes Ward [2] we may call Marduk. She is drawn as a composite and terrifying quadruped with the head, shoulders and fore-limbs of a lion, a body covered with scaly feathers, two wings, the hind legs like those of an eagle, and a protruding, deeply forked tongue like that of a snake. In another glyph a goddess sits on a similar beast, holding the 'lightning trident.' A third cylinder-design exhibits such a beast standing on its hind legs and with open mouth over a kneeling man. A curious feature of all these representations is that a second, smaller dragon always appears, running along on all fours like a dog, the meaning of which remains unexplained. Another figure, reproduced by Maspero, and said to represent Nergal, an underworld agent of war and pestilence, shows him accompanied by many 'devils' combining horrid animal and human features, and also Nergal's consort Ereskigal, a serpent-wielding queen, the ugliest picture of a woman imaginable. Nergal has here the body, fore-limbs and tail of a big, square-headed dog, four wings, the under and foremost two being small and roundish, while the posterior pair reach back beyond the creature's rump like the shards of a beetle; the body is scaly, and the hind legs have the shape of an eagle's. Perhaps what follows will help us to interpret this ugly composition.

All these art-efforts and their like belong to the earliest period, when southern Babylonia was in possession of the Sumerians. Later a different (Semitic) people from the north and west of them became occupants and rulers of Mesopotamia, and we find among their relics at Nineveh and elsewhere seal-cylinders bearing pictures of the conflict between the warrior-god, Bel-Marduk, and the evil genius of the universe, in which the latter is always being struck at, put to flight or killed.

Afterwards in Assyria such figures were grandly drawn, always with a serpentiform head surmounted by two sharp horns, as in that alabaster slab found in the palace of Ashurbanipal at Nimrud, where a storm-god, wielding tridents, fights the traditional monster. "The horned dragon," says Jastrow,[3] "from being the symbol of Enlil . . . becomes the animal of Marduk and subsequently of Ashur as the head of the Assyrian pantheon." These horns long persisted as a royal mark in memory of the fact that Enlil, as Ea, and afterward Marduk, subjugated Tiamat, showing that the conquering dynasty of Ashur assumed their glory and attributes as part of the spoil.

In subsequent and more cultured times an artistically conventionalized image, retaining all the essential elements required by religious tradition, was devised to represent the Evil Spirit, as is shown by the really elegant coloured and glazed tiles that ornament the exterior walls of the magnificent Gate of Ishtar, the approach to the sacred area of Marduk's temple in the ruins of ancient Babylon, an approach built by Nebuchadnezzar four hundred and seventy-five years before the Christian era. Here the dragon reaches its glorification in Assyria, as, in another way, it attained artistic eminence in China and Japan; yet here too it holds tenaciously to the original conception, even then thousands of years old, so impressive and persistent was the underlying reason therefor.

DRAGON OF THE ISHTAR GATE OF BABYLON.
Sixth century B.C.

The very earliest representation known, the model so closely adhered to, is the simplest of all, and in its simplicity best reveals its mythical origin. It is an outline cut on an archaic seal found at Susa, in Persia, which unites the head, wings and feet of a bird (the falcon of Horus) with the lioness of Hathor-Sekhet.

Now it is not necessary to assume that ordinary folk in the towns and gardens and pastures beside either of the two great rivers had a full knowledge, or a lively comprehension, of such ideals and co-relations of gods and men as we have traced. The plain farmer, if given by some priest or sheik such an image as a worshipful object, would probably take it to represent a union of his two worst pests—the lion and eagle that ravaged his herds and preyed on his lambs, while his wife would think of it as a combined jackal and hawk, and treasure it as a charm against their raids upon her chicken-yard. The mystical allegory worked out by the philosophers of the time probably escaped them, and still more likely escaped the busy citizens of Memphis, Nippur, or Susa; yet apparently this philosophy is the principle that has vitalized the persistent, although highly variable, idea which is the soul in the dragon.

"The *fundamental element* in the dragon's powers," declares Professor Smith, "is the control of water. Both the benevolent and the destructive aspects of water were regarded as animated by the Dragon, who thus assumed the rôle of Osiris or his enemy Set. But when the attributes of the Water-God became confused with those of the Great Mother and her evil Avatar, the lioness (Sekhet) form of Hathor in Egypt, or in Babylon the destructive Tiamat, became the symbol of disorder and Chaos, the Dragon became identified with her also." This means that all these primeval 'gods' were in nature both good and bad, could be either saints or devils; and certainly they played contradictory rôles in an amazing way—were dragon, dragon-slayer and the weapon employed, all in the same personage. This wonder-beast ranges from Western Europe to the Far East of Asia, and, in the view of a few extremists, even across the Pacific to America. "Although in the different localities a great number of most varied ingredients enter into its composition, in most places where the dragon occurs the substratum of its anatomy consists of a serpent or a crocodile, usually with the scales of a fish for covering, and the feet and wings, and sometimes also the head, of an eagle, falcon, or hawk, and the fore-limbs and sometimes the head of a lion. An association of anatomical features of so unnatural and arbitrary a nature can only mean that all dragons are the progeny of the same ultimate ancestors."

Chapter Two

WANDERINGS OF THE YOUNG DRAGON

ON THE assumption, which seems fair, that the historic traces of the dragon have led us back to Egypt and Babylonia—and very likely would lead us much farther could we penetrate the obscurities of a remoter past—it is fitting to inquire next how we may account for its presence and varied development elsewhere. Two theories oppose one another in respect to the fact that this and other myths, prejudices, and customs that appear alike, not to say identical, are encountered in widely separated regions, often half the globe apart. One theory explains it on the principle of the general uniformity of human nature and methods of thought, that is, namely: that peoples not at all in contact but under like mental and physical conditions will arrive independently at much the same conclusions as to the origin and causes of natural phenomena, will interpret mysteries of experience and imagination, and will meet daily problems of life, much as unknown others do. This is the older view among ethnologists, and in certain broad features it finds much support, as, for example, in the almost universal respect paid to rainfall and the influences supposed to affect this prime necessity.

Contrary to this view, most students, possessing broader information than formerly, now believe that such resemblances —strikingly numerous—are not mere coincidences arising from a postulated unity of human nature, but are the result of a spread of travellers and instruction from centres where new and impressive ideas or useful inventions have arisen. One of the foremost advocates of this theory of the geographical dispersion of myths and culture, as opposed to local independence of origin, is Professor Smith, quoted in the first chapter, whose books [4] have been of much use to me in this connection. The theory does not deny the occasional independent rise of similar notions and practices here and there, but asserts that it alone accounts for all the important cases, particularly the central nature-myths, of which this of the dragon is esteemed the most important. The doctrine derives its main strength from its ability to show that in the very early, virtually prehistoric, times much closer contact and more frequent intercommunication than was formerly known or considered probable existed among primitive peoples all over the inhabited world. Assuming that at the dawn of history the most advanced communities were those of Egypt and Mesopotamia (with Elam), which were certainly in communication with one another both by land and by sea forty or fifty centuries before Christ, let us see how widespread, if at all, was their influence.

That the Egyptians were building large, sea-going ships as early as 2000 B.C. is well known. In them they traded with Crete and Phœnicia (whence the Phœnicians probably first learned the art of navigation) and with western Mediterranean ports. They sailed up and down the Red Sea, exploring Sinai and Yemen; visited Socotra, where grew the dragon-blood tree; went far south along the African shore; searched the Arabian coast, gathering frankincense (said to be guarded in its growth by small winged serpents); and made voyages back and forth between the Red Sea and the ports of Babylonia and Elam on the Persian Gulf. What surprise could there be were records available that these Egyptian mariners or those in the ships of the people about the Gulf of Persia sometimes continued on to India. Indeed Colonel St. Johnston [5] elaborates a theory that not only the Malay Archipelago but the islands of the South Pacific, especially Polynesia, were colonized prehistorically by a stream of immigrants from Africa and India, who crept along the shore of the Indian Ocean, and from island to island in the East Indies, gradually reaching Australia and going on thence to the sea-islands beyond; and he and others believe that they carried with them ancestral ideas of supernatural beings, whence they made for themselves fish-gods and sea-monsters which some ethnologists regard as not only analogues, but descendants, of dragons. It is stoutly held, furthermore, that the religion of the half-civilized tribes of Mexico owes its characteristic features of serpent-worship and dragonlike symbols to the teaching of Asiatic visitors reaching middle America via Polynesia; but this is disputed, and I shall be content to avoid this controversy—also as far as possible serpent-worship *per se*—and confine myself to continental Asia and Europe.

The southwestern part of Persia, or Elam, was inhabited contemporaneously with early Babylonia, if not before, by a people of equal or superior culture, and holding a like religion. Their capital, Susa, was the most important city east of the lofty mountains between them and the valleys of Mesopotamia, and attracted traders and visitors from a great surrounding space. Most numerous, probably, were those from the north, from Iran, the country about the Caspian Sea and the Caucasus Mountains—inhabited by a race that used to be called Aryans; but many came also from Turanic nomads wandering with their cattle in the valley of the Oxus and eastward to the foot of the Hindoo Koosh, and still others from the eastern plains and coast-lands stretching to the Indus valley.

We may suppose these herdsmen and hunters to have been very simple-minded and crude, and their only semblance of religion to have been the rudest fetishism, animated by fear of ghosts and magic. Only the most enterprising among them, or prisoners of war brought back as slaves, would be likely to visit the more educated South, but there they would hear of definite 'gods' with stories behind them of the creation of the world, the gift of precious rain, and of unseen beings of immeasurable power; and they would learn the reason for representing these divine heroes in the forms they saw inscribed on monuments and temples, or in little images given them, thus getting some notion of the philosophy of worship. They would talk of these things by the camp-fire, when they had returned to Iran or Bactria or the Afghan hills, along with their tales of the civilization in Susa, and gradually plainsmen and mountaineers would grow wiser and more imitative. Sailors and merchants also carried enlightening information and ideas, crude as they may seem to us, into the minds of the natives of the shores of India and along the banks of the navigable Indus, whence this news from the West percolated into the more or less savage interior of the peninsula. Later we shall meet with some results of this slow and accidental propaganda.

Meanwhile, a stronger influence was affecting the North-Persians. Soon after we first become acquainted with the Sumerians settled in Ur and other places on the lower Euphrates, we learn that they were conquered by Semitic tribes from the West, who created the Babylonian empire. After a while this was overthrown by still more powerful forces higher up the

31

river, until finally the Assyrians became rulers of the whole valley, and ultimately of all Asia Minor north of the Arabian desert. The ancient gods received new names, but the old ideas remained. The antique dragon still stood at the gates of the Assyrian king's palace, and Ea, the fish-god, reappeared on the shores of the Mediterranean as Dagon of the Philistines. But this is running ahead of my story.

North of Assyria, among the mountains of Armenia, dwelt the Medes, a nation of uncertain affinities, but apparently well advanced towards civilization even in the earlier period of Babylon's history. They were not, at least primitively, influenced much by the sea-born myths of their southern neighbours, but held a religious creed combined of sun-worship and reverence for serpents—a conjunction which has had many examples elsewhere.

There was born among them, according to good authorities, about a thousand years before Jesus, a man of good family, now called Zoroaster; but others believe he arose in Bactria, and probably at a much older time. He became the founder of a sect holding far higher ideas than those of any of the religious leaders about them. His sect was called Fire-Worshippers, because it kept fires burning perpetually on its altars as a symbol of the pure life believed to be received constantly from the supreme source of life and prosperity, Ormuzd, the All-Wise. It was thus a reform movement rather than a new religion, and inherited a stock of Medic practices and Vedic legends. Its founders and early communicants were evidently in close contact with the people of northern India many centuries before the era of Buddha or Christ, and were trying to elevate religious ideas which were based on faith in the endless conflict between powers classed as helpful to man or injurious to his interests, so that the same gods might be good at one time and bad at another. "Zoroaster established a criterion other than usefulness to determine whether a power was good or bad, by making an ethical distinction between the spirits." Thus the old nature-gods were still recognized but re-classified on a new spiritual and ethical basis; yet they shrank into subordinate rank beside the Wise Spirit Ormuzd, who was in no sense a nature-god but "spirit only and withal the spirit of truth, purity, and justice." These refined ideas gradually sank, however, into the meaner old religion that underlay them; and in opposition to Ormuzd, the personification of All Good, arose a host combined of all the old malicious spirits and influences (demons), led by a supreme personification of Evil called by Zoroaster Lie-Demon, who afterward "becomes the Hostile or Harmful Spirit, Angra Mainyu, Ahriman" of Persian writings. "Among the beings opposed to Ormuzd a conspicuous place is taken by the dragon, Azhi Dahaka, whose home is in Bapel (Babylon) a 'druj,' half-human, half-beast, with three heads. . . . This dragon creates drouth and disease." Here we have recovered the trail of the figure we have been studying, and find him travelling eastward with the mark of Babylon still upon him.

The most ancient writings that have come down to us are the *Vedas*—poems, fables, and allegories recorded in ancient Sanscrit perhaps a dozen centuries before the beginning of the Christian era. They picture weather phenomena as a series of battles fought by a god, Indra, armed with lightnings and thunder, against Azhi, the evil genius of the universe, who has carried off certain benevolent goddesses described allegorically as 'milch-cows,' and who keeps them captive in the folds of the clouds. This fiend was described as a serpent, not because that reptile in life was subtle and crafty, but because he seeks to envelop the goddess of light, the source of the blessed rain, with coils of clouds as with a snake's folds. In the *Gathas* and *Yasnas*, or earliest sacred writings of Persia, preceding the *Avesta*, the 'Bible' of the Zoroastrians, it is asserted that Trita smote Azhi before Indra killed the "monster that kept back the waters." It is a theory of many primitive peoples that an eclipse of the sun or moon means that a celestial monster is swallowing the luminary: the Sumatrans say it is a big snake. Even at this day in China "ignorant folk at the beginning of an eclipse throw themselves on their knees and beat gongs and drums to frighten away the hungry devil." The moon and rainfall are very closely connected in many mythologies.

The forms and characters in which the sky-war appears are almost innumerable as one reads the mythologic narratives of India and Persia; even the summary sketched in his *Zoological Mythology* (Chapter V), by Angelo de Gubernatis, is bewildering in its changes of persons and scenes and methods, involving an exuberance of imagery in which may be discerned the roots of many an attribute characterizing the dragon-stories of long-subsequent times, such as their guarding of treasure, or kidnapping of women, or the grotesque horror of their appearance. And it was all a matter of weather and of the preciousness of rain in a thirsty land!

Superstition went so far as to imagine that human beings of malignant temper might adopt the character and functions of these celestial mischief-makers. It is related in the book *Si-Yu-Ki*, written by Hiuen Tsang, the famous Chinese traveller of the 7th century A.D. (Beal's translation), that in the old days, a certain shepherd provided the king with milk and cream. "Having on one occasion failed to do so, and having received a reprimand, he proceeded . . . with the prayer that he might become a destructive dragon." His prayer was answered affirmatively, and he betook himself to a cavern whence he intended to ravish the country. Then Tathagata, moved by pity, came from a long distance, persuaded the dragon to behave well, and himself took up his abode in the cavern.

Having interpolated this incident, it may be pardonable to give another, extracted from the *Buddhist Records,* illustrating how Buddhist influences tended to modify the fierceness in Brahmanic teachings when they had penetrated the minds of Hindoos dwelling in the valley of the Indus, where, probably, the doctrines of the gentle saint began first to get a foothold in India. The lower valley of that river was visited in 400 A.D., by the Chinese traveller Fa-Huan, who reported that he found at one place a vast colony of male and female disciples:

A white-eared dragon is the patron of this body of priests. He causes fertilizing and seasonable showers of rain to fall within this country, and preserves it from plagues and calamities, and so causes the priesthood to dwell in security. The priests in gratitude for these favours have erected a dragon-chapel, and within it placed a resting-place for his accommodation [and] provide the dragon with food. . . . At the end of each season of rain the dragon suddenly assumes the form of a little serpent both of whose ears are edged with white. The body of priests, recognizing him, place in the midst of his lair a copper vessel full of cream; and then . . . walk past him in procession as if to pay him greeting. He then suddenly disappears. He makes his appearance once every year.

Let us now return to our proper path from this Indian excursion. The Persian Azhi, or Ashi Dahaka, is described in *Yasti IX* as a "fiendish snake, three-jawed and triple-headed, six-eyed, of thousand powers and of mighty strength, a lie-demon of the Daevas, evil for our settlements, and wicked, whom the evil spirit Angra Mainyu made." Darmesteter asserts that the original seat of the Azhi myth was on the southern shore of the Caspian Sea. He says that Azhi was the 'snake' of the storm-cloud, and is the counterpart of the Vedic Ahi or Vritra. "He appears still in that character in *Yasti XIX* seq., where he is described struggling against Atar (Fire) in the sea Vourukasha. His contest with Yima Khshaeta bore at first the same mythological character, the 'shining Yima' being originally, like the Vedic Yima, a solar hero: when Yima was turned into an earthly king Azhi underwent the same fate." He became then the symbol of the enemies of Iran, first the hated Chaldeans and later the Arabs who persecuted the Zoroastrians. A well-known poem of Firdausi relates the legend of how Ahriman in disguise kisses the shoulders of Zohak, a knight who is Azhi in human form, from which kiss sprang venomous serpents. These are replaced as fast as destroyed, and must be fed on the brains of men. In the end Zohak is seized and chained to a rock, where he perishes beneath the rays of the sun. "Fire is everywhere the deadly foe of these 'fiendish' serpents, which are water-spirits; they are ever powerless against the sun, as was Azhi, lacking wit, against Ormuzd."

Such were the notions and faiths regarding dragons as expressed in the earliest written records we possess of philosophy and imagery among Aryan folk; and they floated down the stream of time, remembered and trusted as generation after generation of these simple-minded, poetic people succeeded one another and gradually wandered away from their northern homes to become conquerors and colonists in Iran and India. Let us note certain stories in modern Persian history and literature exhibiting this survival of the ancient ideas.

In his narrative of his travels in Persia, published in London in 1821, Sir William Ouseley [6] relates that in his time there stood near Shiraz the remains of a once mighty castle called Fahender after its builder, a son of the legendary king Ormuz (or Hormuz). This prince rebelled against his brother on the throne and took possession of Fars, with help from the Sassanian family, long before the founding of Shiraz in the 7th century A.D. The castle was repeatedly ruined and repaired as the centuries progressed, and local wiseacres maintain that in it are buried royal arms, treasures, and jewels hidden by the ancient kings, and these are guarded by a talisman. "Tradition adds another guardian to the precious deposit —a dragon or winged serpent; this sits forever brooding over the treasures which it cannot enjoy; greedy of gold, like those famous griffins that contended with the ancient Arimaspians."

This term 'Arimaspian' seems to have been a name among the more settled people of Persia for the more or less nomadic tribes of the plains and mountains west of them, who in subsequent times, nearer the beginning of our era, are seen following one another in great waves of conquering migration from the steadily drying pastures of what we now call Kurdistan westward to the steppes of southern Russia. The earliest of these known as a definite nation were the Cimmerians, who perhaps reached their special country north of the sea of Azov by migration across the mountains of Armenia and the Caucasus. These were followed and replaced by the Scythians, and they in turn were driven out or absorbed by the Sarmatians.

The area they occupied successively north of the Black Sea has been explored by Russian archaeologists, who find that during several centuries previous to the Christian era a substantial though crude civilization existed there, and the worship, or at least a respect for, the snake-dragon prevailed among these peoples. The writings of Prof. M. Rostovtzeff make these investigations accessible to English readers. The dragon-relics discovered make it evident that the notions relating to this matter preserved among the barbarians and peasantry of north-central Europe, which we shall encounter later, were largely derived from these proto-Russians, especially the Sarmatians; and also that they influenced the ideas of the dragon that we shall find in China, with which these early people of the western plains were in constant communication by way of Turkestan, Thibet and Mongolia.

Thus Osvald Sirén, author of *Chinese Art,* in speaking of very early Chinese sculptures, and especially of dragon-figures, remarks:

It seems evident that these dragons are of Sarmatian origin. Their enormous heads and claws are sometimes translated into pure ornaments; their tails into rhythmic curves like the ornamental dragons on the runic stones in Gotland. These two great classes of ornamental dragons, the Chinese and the Scandinavian, are no doubt descendants from the same original stock, which may have had its first period of artistic procreation in western Asia. The artistic ideals of the northern Wei dynasty remained preponderant in Chinese sculpture up to the sixth century (A.D.).

In his famous epic the *Shah Nameh,* translated by Atkinson, Firdausi describes the wondrous adventures of the Persian hero Rustem, who like Hercules had to perform seven labours. At the third stage of this task he was alone in a wilderness with his magical horse Rakush, and lay down to sleep at night, after turning the horse loose to graze. Presently a great dragon came out of the forest. "It was eighty yards in length, and so fierce that neither elephant nor demon nor lion ever ventured to pass by its lair." As it came forth it saw and attacked the horse, whose resistance awakened Rustem; but when Rustem looked around nothing was visible—the dragon had vanished and the horse got a scolding. Rustem went to sleep again. A second time the vision frightened Rakush, then vanished. The third time it appeared the faithful horse "almost tore up the earth with its heels to rouse his sleeping master." Rustem again sprang angrily to his feet, but at that moment sufficient light was providentially given to enable him to see the prodigious cause of the horse's alarm.

> *Then swift he drew his sword and closed in strife*
> *With that huge monster.—Dreadful was the shock*
> *And perilous to Rustem, but when Rakush*
> *Perceived the contest doubtful, furiously*
> *With his keen teeth he bit and tore among*
> *The dragon's scaly hide; whilst, quick as thought,*
> *The champion severed off the grisly head,*
> *And deluged all the plain with horrid blood.*

Another hero of popular legend woven into his history by Firdausi was Isfendiar (son of King Gushtask, himself a dragon-killer), who also had to perform seven labours, the second of which was to fight an enormous and venomous dragon such as this:

Fire sparkles round him; his stupendous bulk
Looks like a mountain. When incensed his roar
Makes the surrounding country shake with fear.
White poison foam drips from his hideous jaws,
Which, yawning wide, display a dismal gulf,
The grave of many a hapless being, lost
Wandering amidst that trackless wilderness.

Isfendiar's companion, Kurugsar, so magnified the power and ferocity of the beast, which he knew of old, that Isfendiar thought it well to be cautious, and therefore had constructed a closed car on wheels, on the outside of which he fastened a large number of pointed instruments. To the amazement of his admirers he then shut himself within this armoured chariot, and proceeded towards the dragon's haunt. Listen to Firdausi:

. . . Darkness now is spread around,
        No pathway can be traced;
The fiery horses plunge and bound
        Amid the dismal waste.

And now the dragon stretches far
        His cavern-throat, and soon
Licks the horses and the car,
        And tries to gulp them down.

But sword and javelin sharp and keen,
        Wound deep each sinewy jaw;
Midway remains the huge machine
        And chokes the monster's maw.

40

And from his place of ambush leaps,
And brandishing his blade,
The weapon in the brain he steeps,
And splits the monster's head.

But the foul venom issuing thence,
Is so o'erpowering found,
Isfendiar, deprived of sense,
Falls staggering to the ground.

As for the dragon—

In agony he breathes, a dire
Convulsion fires his blood,
And, struggling ready to expire,
Ejects a poison flood.

And thus disgorges wain and steeds.
And swords and javelins bright;
Then, as the dreadful dragon bleeds,
Up starts the warrior knight.

Chapter Three

INDIAN NAGAS AND DRACONIC PROTOTYPES

AT A very early period northern India acquired a mixed population composed of conquerors and more peaceful immigrants
from the west and north, which became amalgamated with
whatever remained in the previous inhabitants; and an antique
form of Sanscrit spoken by the invaders became the general
language. They appear, as far back as they can be traced, to
have been an agricultural and cattle-breeding people, using
horses, settled mainly in towns and villages, and considerably
advanced towards civilization. Their religious ideas, at least
within the millennium next preceding the beginning of the
Christian era, as we learn from the *Vedas,* were expressed in
a mythology of nature-gods related to the sun and sky and,
especially to the weather as affecting grass and crops, with
which was mixed a very ancient and fetishistic serpent-worship.
In short these ancestral Hindoos much resembled in ideas the
people of Elam and Chaldea with whom they were already in
communication, but far exceeded them in their reverence of
serpents—naturally, perhaps, as these are more numerous and
dangerous in India than in Mesopotamia.

Their particular object in serpent-veneration was the deadly
cobra, called *naga;* and every one of these hooded reptiles was
regarded as the living incarnation or representative of a great
and fearful company of mythological nagas. These were demi-

gods in various serpentine forms, uncertain of temper and fear-ful in possibilities of harm, whose 'kings' lived in luxury in magnificent palaces in the depths of the sea or at the bottom of inland lakes. They were also said to inhabit an underworld (Patala Land), and were believed to control the clouds, pro-duce thunderstorms, guard treasures, and do weird and mar-vellous things in general. Many feats were attributed to them which could be performed only by beings having human powers and faculties, whence they were said to assume human form from time to time; and stories are told in the writings of 'naga-people' appearing mysteriously and then escaping to the depths of the ocean—probably developed from incidents in which wild strangers had raided the coast and when discovered had fled over the horizon in their boats. The ruder tribes, which were most addicted to cobra-worship, and were despised by the Brahmanic class, were known as Naga men or simply Nagas. This cult persists in remote districts to this day, and is espe-cially vigorous in the rough country of northern Burma and Siam, where temples of snake-worship are yet maintained. Doubtless it formerly prevailed beyond India all over the Malay Peninsula and among the unknown aborigines of China.

It must be remembered in connection with these facts that the semi-civilized inhabitants of the Northwest were largely a maritime people. Living along the great Indus River they early took to the sea and became daring navigators, voyaging far eastward on both plundering and trading expeditions. The civilization of both Burma and Indochina, according to Old-ham's investigations, is shown by history as well as legend to be owing to invaders from India, who introduced there not only ideas of a settled life and trade, but taught the notions of naga-worship, and later Buddhistic doctrines and practices throughout southern China, Java, Sumatra and Celebes. Buddha himself refers to such voyages, in which no doubt religious missionaries sometimes participated.

Mingled with this was direct teaching from Babylon and Egypt, as has already been mentioned. "Within twenty years of the introduction of the Phœnician navy into the Persian Gulf by Sennacherib traders from the Red Sea arrived in the gulf of Kiao-Chau, and soon established colonies there." This was in the middle of the sixth century B.C. "They came on ships bearing bird or animal heads and two big eyes on the bow, and two large steering-oars at the stern—distinctly Egyptian methods of ship-building."

Into the Vedic civilization of northern India, was introduced, about the seventh century B.C., the more spiritual and unselfish cult of Buddhism. Its most difficult problem was the overcoming of cobra-worship, and as this proved impossible, the Buddhists were compelled to be content with trying to improve the worst features of ophiolatry among the Naga tribes; but this conciliatory attitude seems to have led to a weakening and corruption of the gospel preached by Buddha and his first apostles. Legends, though conflicting, indicate this. It is related, for example, that a naga king foretold the attainment of Gautama to Buddhahood; and the cobra-king who lived in Lake Mucilinda sheltered Lord Buddha for seven days from wind and rain by his coils and spreading hoods, as is represented in many antique pictures and sculptures. At any rate a schism developed over this matter, resulting in the southern Buddhists teaching less strict doctrine with reference to the old beliefs, which became known as the Manhayana school.

The nagas' ability to raise clouds and thunder when out of

temper was cleverly absorbed by this school into the highly beneficent power of giving rain to thirsty earth, and so these dreadful beings became by the influence of Buddha's 'Law' blessers of men. "In this garb," as Dr. Visser [7] points out, "they were readily identified with the Chinese dragons, which were also beneficent rain-gods of water"; and it was this modified, semi-Hindoo, Manhayana conception of Buddhism, with its tolerance of serpent-divinity, which was carried by wandering missionaries and traders during the later Han period into China and eastward.

Visser ascertained, in his profound examination of this serpent-cult, that in later Indian, that is Greco-Buddhist, art, the nagas appear as real dragons, although with the upper part of the body human. "So we see them on a relief from Gandahara, worshipping the Buddha's alms-bowl in the shape of big water-dragons, scaled and winged, with two horse-legs, the upper part of the body human." They may be found represented even as men or women with snakes coming out of their necks and rising over their heads, which recalls the prime fiends of Persian legend, and also the prehistoric pictures of the more or less mythical Chinese sage Fu Hsi.

The four classes into which the Indian Manhayanists divided their nagas were (quoting Visser):

Heavenly Nagas—who uphold and guard the heavenly palace.
Divine Nagas—who cause clouds to rise and rain to fall.
Earthly Nagas—who clear out and drain off rivers, opening outlets.
Hidden Nagas—guardians of treasures.

This corresponds closely with Professor Cyrus Adler's list (*Report U. S. National Museum,* 1888), of the four kinds of

Chinese dragons: "The early cosmogonists enlarged on the imaginary data of previous writers and averred that there were distinct kinds of dragons proper—the *t'ien-lung* or celestial dragon, which guards the mansions of the gods and supports them so that they do not fall; the *shen-lung* or spiritual dragon, which causes the winds to blow and produces rain for the benefit of mankind; the *ti-lung* or dragon of the earth, which marks out the courses of rivers and streams; and the *fu-ts'ang-lung* or dragon of hidden treasures, which watches over the wealth concealed from mortals. Modern superstition has further originated the idea of four dragon kings, each bearing rule over one of the four seas which form the borders of the habitable earth."

In a Tibetan picture referred to by Visser nagas are depicted in three forms: Common snakes guarding jewels; human beings with four snakes in their necks; and winged sea-dragons, the upper part of the body human, but with a horned, ox-like head, the lower part of the body that of a coiling dragon. This shows how a queer mixture of Chaldean, Persian and Hindoostanee elements reached Tibet by very ancient caravan roads north of the Himalayan ranges; and it throws light on one possible origin of the four-legged figure adopted by the

ANCESTORS OF THE DRAGON.
(See footnote on facing page.)

Chinese, especially in the northern marches of the empire where the inhabitants were open to Bactrian, Scythian, and other western influences.

That composite animal-form of the rain-god of the Euphrates people, the horned sea-goat of Marduk (immortalized as the Capricornus of our Zodiac), was also the vehicle of Varuna in India, whose relationship to Indra was in some respects analogous to that of Ea to Marduk in Babylonia. In his account of Sanchi and its ruins General Maisey, as quoted by Smith, states that: "As to the fish-incarnation of Vishnu and Sakya Buddha, and as to the makara, dragon or fish-lion, another form of which was the naga of the waters, the use of the symbol by both Brahmans and Buddhists, and their common use of the sacred barge, are proofs of the connection between both forms of religion and the far older myths of Egypt and Assyria." Havell [8] is of the opinion that the crocodile-dragon which appears in the figure of Siva dancing in the great temple of Tanjore, may have been older than the eleventh century when the temple was built. "In the earlier Indian rendering of this sun-symbolism, as seen in the Buddhist 'horse-shoe' arches," says Havell, "the crocodile-dragon, the demon of darkness, who swallows the sun at night and releases it in the morning, is not combined with these sun-windows until after the development of the Manhayana school."

Sun-worship, serpent-worship, phallicism, and dragons are inextricably interwoven in Oriental mythology.

It is in the Indian makara, I think, that we have the 'link' between the Western conception and that of the Chinese as to the shape of this fabulous water-spirit. Yet, all the makaras of Vedic myth are simply a crocodile in simple form, or else are variants of Marduk's sea-goat with two front feet only, varied according to the head and body into antelopes (black-buck), cats, elephants, etc., all carrying fish-tails. The Chinese dragon, on the other hand, has nothing of the fish about it, but is wholly serpent, except its horned and fantastic head and the fact that it invariably possessed (crocodile-like) four legs and feet which are quite as like those of a bird as like those of a lion. There is evidently some significance in the bird-like feet. Can they be a relic of the introduction ages ago of the Babylonian or Elamite figure of the rain-god, composed by joining the symbols of Hathor-Sekhet and Horus? That is to say, do they possibly represent the long-forgotten falcon of the bright son of Osiris?

"In Chinese Buddhism," Dr. Anderson informs us in his celebrated *Catalogue,* "the dragon plays an important part either as a fierce auxiliary to the Law or as a malevolent crea-ture to be converted or quelled. Its usual character, however, is that of a guardian of the faith under the direction of Buddha, Bodhisattvas, or Arhats. As a dragon king it officiates at the baptism of the Sakyamuni, or bewails his entrance into Nir-vana; as an attribute of saintly or divine personages it appears at the feet of the Arhat Panthaka, emerging from the sea to salute the goddess Kuanyin, or as an attendant upon or alterna-tive form of Sarasvati, the Japanese Benten; as an enemy of mankind it meets its Perseus and Saint George in the Chinese monarch Kao Tsu (of the Han dynasty) and the Shinto god Susano'no Mikoto. When this religion made its way into China, where the hooded snake was unknown, the emblems shown in the Indian pictures and graven images lost their force of suggestion, and hence became replaced by a mythical but more familiar emblem of power."

It was mainly—but not altogether, as we shall see—from

Indian sources that the now familiar four-footed dragon of China became conventialized through its applications in the several arts of decoration and devotion; and it seems a fair inference that the aggressive Buddhist influence of the early centuries of that sect led Chinese artists to change the smooth, well-proportioned *ch'ih-lung* of their forefathers, chin-bearded like the ancient sages, into a sort of jungle python with the horrifying head and face characteristic of the countenances of antique Buddhistic images of their demons. To understand how inhumanly terrible these caricatures of malignant beings in the guise of humanity may be, one need only glance at drawings of the temple images exhumed by Sir Aurel Stern from the sand-buried Indo-Chinese cities of Turkestan, which flourished about the time of which I am speaking.

Buddhist artists, at first probably aliens, would be likely to depict the dragon head and face in their attempts to portray the chief 'demon', as they mistakenly regarded the friendly Chinese divinity, after the same horrifying fashion. Then, to impress the people of the North, who saw few dangerous snakes, but who did know and fear tigers and leopards, the artists equipped their frightful-headed serpent with catlike legs, bird's feet, such tufts of hair as decorate and would suggest a lion, and a novel ridge of iguana-like spines along its backbone.

The fully realized dragon, then, as we see it in bronzes or sprawled across a silken screen, is an invention of decorative artists striving, during the last 2000 years, to embody a traditional but essentially foreign idea.

Chapter Four

THE DIVINE SPIRIT OF THE WATERS

TODAY, WHEN one hears the word 'dragon' one's mind almost inevitably pictures the fantastic figure embroidered in red and gold thread on some gorgeous Chinese garment, or winding its clouded way about the lustrous curves of a Japanese vase. To Western eyes it is hardly more than a quaint conventionalized ornament, but to Orientals, let me repeat, it is an embodiment of all the significance of national history and ancient philosophy—the natural and supreme symbol of their race and culture. Again, the Western man looks on the dragon as something as mythical as the Man in the Moon, but the great mass of the people in China, Tibet, and Korea, at least, believe in the *lung* (its ancient name) as now alive, active and numerous —believe in it with as firm and simple a faith as our infants put in the existence of Santa Claus, or the Ojibway in his Thunder Bird, or you and I in the law of gravitation. "The legends of Buddhism abound with it; Taoist tales contain circumstantial accounts of its doings; the whole countryside is filled with stories of its hidden abodes, its terrific appearances; . . . its portrait appears in houses and temples, and serves even more than the grotesque lion as an ornament in architecture, art-designs and fabrics." So testifies one who knew!

It is generally agreed that the original Chinese came in from the plateaus west and north of the Yellow River by following its sources down to the plains. This river takes its name (Hoang-Ho) from the hue of its soil-laden current, and that may account, in connection with the golden tint of the venerated sun's light, for the supremacy of yellow in Chinese mythology and political history: it is the national as it was the imperial color until the yellow dragon-flag of the senile empire fell beneath the stripes of the young Republic.

Everywhere the dragon, when first heard of, is associated with the genesis of the arts of civilization in China. Myths relating to it go back to the thirty-third century before Christ, and to the sage Fu Hsi who then (or, as some say, between 2853 and 2738 B.C.) dwelt in the Province of Honan, and from whom dates the legendary as distinguished from a mythical period before him.

One day Fu Hsi saw a yellow 'dragon-horse'—a horse-headed water-beast of some sort—rise from the Lo River, a tributary of the Hoang Ho, marked on its back with an arrangement of curling hairs expressing somehow those mysterious Trigrams that have survived for the puzzlement of scholars, but are generally considered as the formula or apparatus of a system of prehistoric divination based on mathematics—the theory of the symbolic quality of numbers so widespread and influential in the ancient East. The Trigrams are expounded in that book of unknown antiquity, the *Yi King,* which is the Bible of the Taoists, and seem to form an attempt at graphic demonstration of the mystical principle at the heart of Chinese philosophy expressed in the terms 'yang' and its antithesis 'yin'. We shall meet these contrasted terms wherever our search may lead us, and shall learn that the sages have found in them, as DeGroot,[9] the foremost expositor of Chinese theology, ex-

PORCELAIN JAR WITH 'DRAGON HORSE.'
Japanese, eighteenth century.
Courtesy of the Metropolitan Museum.

PORCELAIN JAR WITH DRAGON.
Chinese, sixteenth century.

ANCIENT DRAGON PILLARS.

Chinese, fourth century. Courtesy of the Smithsonian
Institution.

presses it, a "clue to the mysteries of nature and an unfathomable lake of metaphysical wisdom."

Be this as it may, the dragon-horse is a strange feature of the history of our subject, and one still among the possibilities of vision to the eyes of the faithful. A native commentary on one of the Classics, written in the second century B.C., and consulted by Dr. Visser, informs its readers that a dragon-horse is the vital spirit of heaven and earth fused together. "Its shape consists of a horse's body, yet it has dragon-scales. Its height is eight ch'ih, five ts'un. A true dragon-horse has wings at its sides and walks upon the water without sinking. If a holy man is on the throne it comes out of the midst of the Ming River carrying a map [i.e., the Trigrams] on its back." Wang Fu, another author of early Han times, says: "The people paint the dragon's shape with a horse's head and a snake's tail. Further, there are such expressions as 'three joints' and 'nine resemblances,' to wit, from head to shoulder, from shoulder to breast, from breast to tail." The nine resemblances referred to seem to indicate nine kinds of animals, parts of which are combined in this imaginary beast. Another description mentions particularly a tail like that of a huge serpent; and Wang Kia asserts in his book, written A.D. 557, that Emperor Muh, of the Chow dynasty, once "drove around the world in a carriage drawn by eight winged dragon-horses." Some kings saddled and rode these prototypes of the classic Pegasus. Certainly horse-like figures with queer little feathery wings and upturned feathery tails appear in art produced under the Han dynasty, and later one finds drawings or sculptures of them showing well-developed wings. Visser quotes a reference, as late as 741 A.D., to the appearance, somewhere in China, of a living blue-and-red example that was heard "neighing like a flute." The dragon-horse is known in Japanese folklore also.

It seems to me very natural and interesting that these earliest recoverable notions of the aspect of the dragon should have conceived of it as having an equine form, reminiscent of the primitive home and habits of the ancestors of these adventurers in the Hoang-Ho Valley in whose nomadic life horses had borne so essential a part; and it is further interesting to observe that in Tibet representations of the dragon, with little resemblance otherwise to the conventional Chinese model, have the legs and hoofs of the horse instead of those of the lion or the eagle.

Recalling the significance attached by some native commentators to the strange markings on the back of the equine creature which legend says appeared before the sage Fu Hsi, that, namely, they taught him the making and use of the ideographic characters by which Chinese is written, it is worth while to mention a tradition of the legendary emperor Tsang Kie, to whose reign is popularly attributed the introduction of writing as well as other inventions of importance. "One day, the emperor, surrounded by his principal ministers, was thinking of . . . how much had been accomplished, when an immense dragon descended from the clouds, and placed itself at his feet. The emperor, and those who had assisted him in his wonderful discoveries, got upon the reptile's back, which forthwith took its flight to celestial regions." Several early Buddhist heroes and worthies were similarly translated.

The interesting point of resemblance in these legends is that they agree in making the knowledge of writing a divine gift—a fact most appropriate to the pride of the Chinese in literary accomplishments.

The earliest example known to me of a dragon in recognizable Chinese form is shown on some ancient pillars in the city of Yung-Ch'eng near Tientsin.

During an archaeological survey of the coastal district of southern Shansi province, China, wherein much of the earliest history and tradition of the Chinese has its source, Dr. Chi Li was led to inspect certain old temples in the city of Yun-Ch'eng, a brief note on which appears in "The Explorations and Field Work of the Smithsonian Institution in 1926," accompanied by the photograph which the Institution has generously allowed me to reproduce here. Dr. Li's account is as follows:

In "Shansi-t'ung-chih" (Vol. 52, p. 2) it is recorded that the stone pillars of these temples were formerly the palace pillars of Wei Hui-wang (335–370 A.D.), recovered from the ruined city south of An-i Hsien. Some of them are now used as the entrance pillars in Ch'en-huang Miao and Hou-t'u Miao, and those of Ch'en-huang Miao certainly show peculiar features which are worth recording. Two pillars, hexagonal in section, and carved with dragons coiled around them, are found at the entrance. The left one is especially interesting because in the claws of the dragon are clasped two human heads with perfect Grecian features: curly hair, aquiline and finely chiselled nose, small mouth and receding cheeks. One head with the tongue sticking out is held at the mouth of the dragon, while the other is held in the talons of one hind leg. It is an unusually fine piece of sculpture in limestone. . . . I saw 28 of this kind of pillar in the succeeding two days; but most of them were imitations. It is possible, however, that some are of the ancient type and were made earlier than others. The whole subject is well worth more detailed study.

This brief account (which comes while the book is in the

hands of the printer so that the facts may not be further elucidated here), is of particular interest as one of the earliest representations of the creature we are studying after it had begun to take its modern shape. Here it has a more naturally crocodilian form, especially as to the head, which has not yet acquired the fantastically frightful shape and appendages given it by later artists. It is also notable that the precious flaming 'pearl,' so important a feature in all modern figures, is already associated with this statue of fifteen centuries ago.

A very ancient bit of folklore, which accounts for the birth of the dragon in the form in which we now know it, was found in the archives of Weihaiwei, in Shantung, by R. F. Johnston, and is recorded in his book [10] as follows:

The legend current in Weihaiwei regarding the origin of the dragon-king (who may be compared with the naga-raja of the Indian Peninsula) runs somewhat as follows: His mother was an ordinary mortal, but gave birth to him in a manner that was not—to say the least—quite customary. Being in his dragon-shape the lusty infant immediately flew away on a journey of exploration, but returned periodically for the purpose of being fed. As he grew larger and more terrifying day by day his mother grew much alarmed, and confided her woes to her husband, the dragon's father. The father after due consideration decided there was no help for it but to cut off his preposterous son's head: so next day he waited behind a curtain, sword in hand, for the dragon's arrival. The great creature flew into the house in his usual unceremonious manner, curled his tail around a beam below the roof, and hung head downwards in such a way that by swaying himself he could reach his mother's breast.

At this juncture his father came from behind the curtain, whirled his sword around his head, and brought it down on what ought to have been the dragon's neck. But whether it was that his hand shook or his prey was too quick for him the fact remains that the dragon's head remained where it was. . . . Before the sword could be whirled a second time the dragon seized his father round the waist, untwisted his tail from the beam in the roof, and flew away to the eastern seas. The dragon's father was never seen again, but the dragon and his mother were elevated to divine rank from which they have never since been displaced. The reasons for elevation to godhead are perhaps not quite apparent: but the popular saying that "the dragon's bounty is as profound as the ocean, and the mother-dragon's virtue is as lofty as the hills," has a reference to their functions as controllers of the rains and clouds.

Passing by various more or less fabulous sources of doubtful information, we come down to the time of the Chow dynasty in the twelfth century, B.C., where begins a fairly trustworthy account of imperial acts. Collections of songs and stories that are older remain, but the most important of ancient literary productions, the five great 'Classics,' were published during the early reigns of this period. "With the Chow founder, the great Wen Wang," writes Professor Ernest Fenollosa, "we are on pretty firm historic ground. This acute personage, whose name means 'king of literature,' was the first great Chinese author and philosopher. It was he who composed in prison the original score of the *Yi King*, or Book of Changes, which Confucius much later elaborated. In this work the symbolism of dragon categories is so bound up with imperial acts as to be the origin of all that is still implied in the terms 'dragon-throne,' 'dragon-face,' 'dragon-banner.' In a sense the dragon is the type of a man self-controlled and with powers that verge on the supernatural."

It must not be forgotten, meanwhile, that these notions are closely connected with that mysterious Chinese conception called *feng-shui,* which from time immemorial has been the ruling influence in determining a large part of personal and public affairs throughout the nation, especially with whatever has to do with disturbance of the ground, fixing a local position (as for a house or a grave), or the supposed celestial influences.

Feng-shui, literally translated, means nothing more than 'wind and (rain-)water,' but these words alone fail to convey its full significance. "It originated," De Groot explains, "in ancient ages from the then prevailing conceptions . . . that the inhabitants of this world all live under the sway of the influences of heaven and earth, and that every one desirous of securing his own felicity must live in perfect harmony with those influences. . . . This reverential awe of the mysterious influences of nature is the fundamental principle of an ancient religious system usually styled by foreigners Taoism [Tao's Way, i.e., path]." Few Chinese even now are enlightened or brave enough to put up any sort of building except in accordance with the theories of feng-shui, which often require childish particulars. Most important is it, for instance, that a grave should have something symbolic of the tiger on its right, or theoretical west side, and of a dragon on the left (east) side, "for these animals represent all that is meant by the word 'feng-shui,' viz: both æolian and aquatic influences." So writes De Groot. Anesaki explains further, in his book on Buddhist art, the reference to the association of dragon and tiger: "In this contending pair the Zenists, a sect of Buddhists, saw a graphic representation of the all-controlling forces which break down terrestrial distinctions and fuse together heaven and earth."

Ball quotes an example of how feng-shui may be troublesome to both European and native attempts at progress in Western fashion. He writes:

In the phraseology of this occult science, when two buildings are beside one another the one on the left is said to be built on the Green Dragon, and the one on the right on the White Tiger. Now the tiger must not be higher than the dragon, or death or bad luck will result. Supposing now a European or American gets a site for a residence next to and on the right-hand side of a native dwelling—here are all the elements ready for trouble, for, to begin with, the foreigner will naturally desire a house more suitable for habitation than the low abode of the average Chinaman.

Feng-shui has well been called China's curse!

In view of the association of dragons with this geomantic superstition it need not surprise us to find that divination and prophecy belong to their powers; but the portents and omens derived from this source depend so much on external conditions and the opinions of soothsayers that no satisfactory rules for consultation seem to exist. Visser learned that the appearance of a black dragon presaged destruction—but who knows a black dragon when he sees it? Traditions report that the advent of certain great men of the past was foretold by dragons. They say that in the night when Confucius was born two azure dragons came from the sky to his mother's house. A dragon appeared in a red vapour just before the birth of Hiao Wu, the famous man of the Han dynasty. The appearance of yellow or azure dragons was always in old times considered a very good omen, provided they did not present themselves at the wrong time or place. Lu Kwang, who lived in the fourth century B.C., saw one night a black horned dragon. "Its eyes illuminated the whole vicinity, so that the huge monster was visible until it was enveloped by the clouds which gathered from all sides. Next morning traces of its scales were to be seen over a distance of five miles, but soon were wiped out by heavy rains." Other ancients have seen similar night-monsters, such as that which shone upon the palace of Shun-shuh, who, became emperor in A.D. 25.

This introduces the pseudo-science, geomancy, which is founded on the almost divine doctrine of feng-shui, and in which the dragon plays a most important part, because it represents the watershed-slopes and foothills as well as the streams that wind their way among them in any locality toward the general outlet. "In short," to quote again from De Groot, "geomancy comprises the high grounds in general: hence many geographical names, such, for example, as Nine Dragons (*Kau Lung*) given to the range of hills opposite Hong Kong known to the English as Kowloon. The apparent contradiction here seems to be adjusted by considering the hills as the source of the watercourses." This identification with water, an all-important element in feng-shui, classifies dragons with the spring, the season of fertilizing rains, and in southern China March is called dragon-month. The relations and symbolism of the seasons and the four quarters of the earth, etc., are as tabulated below:

Spring	East	blue	azure dragon
Summer	South	red	phenix (feng)
Autumn	West	white	tiger
Winter	North	black	tortoise

Here the dragon heads the list of the four 'celestial' or 'intelligent' animals that existed in and made possible the Golden Age.

I find in Dr. Laurence Binyon's delightful little book *The Flight of the Dragon*,[11] a comment illuminating this association of things and ideas:

In Chinese popular tradition there are five colours. These are blue, yellow, red, white, and black. Each of these are linked by tradition with certain associations. Thus blue is associated with the east, red with the south, white with the west, black with the north and yellow with the earth. . . . Blue appears originally not to have been distinguished from green —at least the same word was used for both—and it was associated with the east because of the coming of spring with its green. That black should be associated with the cold north seems more intelligible, and that to the black north would be opposed the red of the fiery south; but that white should belong to the west because autumn comes with the winds from that quarter, heralded by white frosts, seems a far-fetched explanation. .And when we pursue the ulterior significance of the colours into still wider regions; when we find blue associated with wood, red with fire, white with metal, black with water; still more when we are told that the five colours have each correspondences with the emotions (white with mourning, for instance, and black with worry), and not only with these but

61

with musical notes, with the senses and with flavours, I fear the august common-sense of the Occident becomes affronted and impatient.

Preëminent in all this plexus of faiths and fancies is the cardinal fact that the Oriental dragon stands for 'water.'

"If one represents water without representing dragons there is nothing to show the divinity of its phenomena," declared an ancient writer cited by Dr. Visser. Another antique script describes a divine being in the waters of the earth akin to the snake, which sleeps in pools during the winter, whence in spring it ascends to the sky. These mysticisms evidently refer to fresh waters alone (the salt seas are in another class), just as in Ur, Ea, the god of the rain-clouds, and of the streams and lakes they fed, was regarded as quite distinct from oceanic deities; and such reverential ideas must, it would seem, have had their genesis in the minds of people of an arid region whose thoughts were continually on their water-supply. But in the softer circumstances which resulted from their finding homes in the fertile valleys of China they felt the apprehension of drouth less severely, and began to ponder on the reasonableness of their ancient fears and present veneration. "Water," declared Lao Tzu, "is the weakest and softest of things, yet overcomes the strongest and the hardest." It penetrates everywhere subtly, without noise, without effort. "So it becomes typical of the spirit, which is able to pass out into all other existences of the world and resume its own form in man; and, associated with the power of fluidity, the dragon becomes the symbol of the infinite." Water-worship, indeed, is a widespread and very ancient cult, the central idea being that water is the source and means of fertility and also of purification in its higher senses. Hence great rivers have been invested with a sacred character, notably the Nile and the Ganges; even the Yangtse and Hoang rivers have inspired similar sentiments. Plutarch says that Nile water, which fecundated the earth, was carried in processions in honour of Isis as representing the seed of Osiris. The stark necessity of water in the plan of creation and the scheme of life seems to have impressed the primitive man of arid Central Asia with amazing force.

A Chinese author of the third century B. C. assures his readers that mankind cannot see dragons rise, but that wind and rain assist them to attain a great height; another asserts that the dragon does not ascend if there is no wind. Whirlwinds that carry heavy objects aloft, and at sea cause waterspouts, have always been looked upon as dragons winging their way to the upper regions of the air; and smoking holes in the ground connected with volcanic action are said to be holes whence they emerge for their flights. In the beginning of summer, as we are informed by one commentator, the dragons of the world are divided, so that each has a separate territory whose limits he does not pass. This is the reason why in summer it may rain very much at one place and not at all at another not far away.

The dragon is also god of thunder, appearing in the sky as clouds (said by some to be formed of his breath) and in the rice-fields as rain, whence he is worthy of veneration as the power that produces good crops. Sometimes cloud-birds (or bird-clouds) are seen helping him.

Since early times high floods, tempests and ordinary thunderstorms have been attributed by rural Chinese to dragons fighting in the air or in rivers. This is not a blessing to humanity, such as they bestow by peacefully shedding rain on the planted fields, and therefore the threatening 'herds' of dragons advancing to combat were looked at with fright. An account of a dragon-fight in a pool in northern Liang, in 503 B.C., relates that vicious creatures "squirted fog over a distance of some miles." The only way to stop such dreadful duels is by the use of fire, which no water-spirit can endure; therefore heaven sends sacred fire (the lightnings) to compel angry demons to cease troubling the clouds or mundane waters and injuring poor farmers, as all-destroying deluges might result. Hence, occasional small or local damage to mankind, as innocent bystanders, from the vigorous quelling of draconic riots, is regarded as cheap payment for security against overwhelming floods. More dreadful however than immediate storm-damage was the presage in the sky-battles of possible harm to, or even the overthrow of, the reigning family, which almost certainly would follow were the yellow and the blue dragon-hosts, partisans of the Imperial House, to be defeated.

It is true that in primitive China as elsewhere serpents were regarded as the genii of lakes, springs and caves, and here and there the people paid them worship. The dragon, however, is not, nor ever was, an ordinary snake deified, but has been exalted, albeit rather uncertainly, into a true deity as a manifestation of a principle that underlies all Chinese philosophy, and is expressed in the contrasted and pregnant words *yang* and *yin*—light versus darkness, the constructive as opposed to the destructive, goodwill contrasted with badheartedness.

In the *Shan hai King,* a very old Classic, is described a god seated at the foot of Mt. Chung. "He is called 'Enlightener of the Darkness.' By looking [i.e., opening the eyes; a popular belief is that a dragon's vital spirit lies in his eyes, also that

64

he is deaf] he creates daylight, and by closing his eyes he creates night. By blowing he makes winter, by inhalation he makes summer. He neither eats nor drinks, nor does he rest. His breath causes wind. His length is a thousand miles. . . . As a living being he has a human face, the body of a snake, and a red colour."

The author assures us that this god is The Dragon, that he is full of *yang* (heavenly virtue), and that it is logical that he should diffuse light, overcoming the nine *yin;* wherefore he symbolizes great men (assumed to be full of *yang*) particularly the emperor and his sons ('dragon-seed') which is one of the many explanations of the association of the Thunder dragon, specifically the yellow one, with the imperial estate. If this be true—and the possession of *yang* by dragons is affirmed by sages again and again—the good nature of Chinese dragons in general is well accounted for. In China, at any rate, they have been on the whole benevolent and helpful when treated with respect and generously encouraged by sacrifices and gifts. Undoubtedly they have sometimes shown poor judgment in the matter of flooding rains and a careless use of lightning, yet in general they seem to mean well, and to be kind in answer to prayers for rain when the crops really need it. If not—well, the farmers know how to bring them to their sense of duty!

Such an abstraction, precious to devout minds in spite of puzzling characteristics and a vague aspect, must of course be visualized in some way if it is to hold heroic place and influence. "The dragon is the spirit of change," writes Okakoro-Kakuzo in his *Book of Tea,* "therefore of life itself . . . taking new forms according to its surroundings, yet never seen in final shape. It is the great mystery itself. Hidden in the caverns of inaccessible mountains, or coiled in the unfathomed depth of the sea, he awaits the time when he slowly arouses himself into activity. He unfolds himself in the storm-cloud, he washes his mane in the darkness of the seething whirlpools. His claws are the fork of the lightning. . . . His voice is heard in the hurricane. . . . The dragon reveals himself only to vanish."

Chapter Five

DRACONIC GRANDPARENTS

AS SOON as men learn to form, by means of a drawing or an image, a representation of what is in their mind's eye, they apply their art to religion. The first attempts are often grotesquely rude and uninspiring, yet embody an idea; and if the people cherish this idea, and themselves grow in art-skill and refinement, a conventionalized figure will in time be evolved that will satisfy tradition, and thereafter no essential change will be made in it.

Fair progress toward this satisfactory representation of the (or a) dragon, now apparently realized, seems to have been reached by the Chinese at a time when the earliest existing, or at any rate oldest known, pictures and carvings of it were made, nor are any written descriptions much older, so that we may assume a long anterior period for the growth of the dragon-notion in public thought. A few years ago many large inscribed slabs of stone were found buried in Shantung, one of the most anciently occupied provinces of China. They bore engravings in an amazing mixture of more or less legendary incidents and worthies, and experts refer this work to the third century B.C. One of these slabs shows a silhouette-like drawing that we are told represents Fu hsi with a woman regarded as his consort. Both are crowned and fully dressed down to the waist, but the lower half of their bodies is serpent-like (in proportionate length for legs) and the 'tails' are inter-twined. Attendant pairs of sprites of anomalous outline, with tail-like lower halves similarly twisted together, are supported by rolled clouds terminating in birds' heads; and the remaining space of the picture is crowded with figures of mythical creatures, some queer beyond description, many recognizable birds, fishes, or other real animals, all with reptilian tails. Rubbings of these astonishing lithographs are before me as I write, and small reproductions of some of the figures may be seen in Bushell's Handbook of Chinese Art.[12] They, as well as other relics from Han times (earlier than which no useful representations have been recovered), show clearly the ophidian origin of the dragon idea, and also indicate strongly its derival from the West.

It is a curious circumstance that among remains of the earlier Gnostics, whose strange doctrines are credited with descent from Aryan (Persian) serpent-worship, are representations of deities, half man, half snake, precisely similar in shape, save that they have two snake-legs instead of a single thickened tail, as was the case with some of the figures on the stone slabs of Shantung. With the overthrow of the Chow (or Chou) dynasty by the widely conquering 'General' Chin (so impressive were the extent and publicity of his enterprises that his domain came to be known to the commercial West as *China*) the enlightened and progressive Han period began; and in the general stimulus to art that followed, the dragon furnished to artists a motive constantly employed and ingeniously varied. No depiction in painting or on pottery as ancient as that has survived, if any such ever existed. It is surely an interesting fact, however, that the first Chinese painter on record, Ts-ao Fuh-king, who died in 250 A.D., was famous for his Buddhist pictures and sketches of dragons. An oft-told legend recounts that a certain painting by him which had been preserved until the advent of the Sung dynasty, then produced rain in a time of bitter drouth when appealed to by the desperate farmers.

As for Han carvings in this direction, the most striking and exceptional are those strange and beautiful 'girdle-buckles,' which were almost unknown in the United States until Mr. Arthur D. Ficke brought a large collection of them to New York, where they were sold at the Anderson galleries in January, 1925. The work on them, in exquisite modelling, proper anatomy and fine sense of action, and in the glyptic skill involved, indicates a long-antecedent familiarity by artists with both the conception and rendering of the mythical creature portrayed. Most of these articles were carved in jade, a few only in rock-crystal, agate or other hard stone. Mr. Ficke wrote of them in his *Catalogue*:

It would be impossible, in a brief catalogue such as this, to give any intimation of the wealth of symbolic meanings that have been carven into these buckles. The dragon, the hydra, the bat, the fungus, the horse, the mantis, the cicada, the monkey, and the ram, has each its significance in Chinese mythological legend. Some of these forms go back at least two thousand years, repeated over and over again in bronzes and jades of century after century. These fantastic shapes are therefore racial rather than personal inventions: they are the creatures of prehistoric ritual—mythology turned to stone.

Few of these are as old as the Han period, but all remind a naturalist of a salamander by their flexible, soft-skinned bodies, limber legs usually with three toes, and their long, cleft tails. In every specimen the tail is branched. I write 'branched,' not 'forked,' because the lobes are unequal, a shorter one curving out of the larger or main stem—as, by the way, sometimes happens in the case of real newts whose tails have been lost or damaged. This style of dragon is named *ch'ih-lung*, and is said to be pre-Buddhistic (also, according to Bushell, *kut'ing-lung*, or dragon of old bronzes); and he mentions that it appears on a Kuang Yao vase of the second century B.C., while another pair is to be seen on a more recent incense-burner "disporting in the midst of scrolled clouds and projecting their heads to make two handles." It is very interesting to note that although many of the jade girdles are of comparatively recent manufacture, and vary in ornamental details, the newt-like character of the body and branched tail persists. It seems to me, indeed, that the ch'ih-lung represents, as nearly as we can reach it, the primitive dragon-notion that prevailed (at least in northern China) before the Buddhistic invasion from India became widespread and influential in the country, and that it came overland from the northwest.

Dr. Berthold Laufer [13] describes an antique jade girdle-ornament which had "the figure of a phenix standing on clouds and looking toward the slender-bodied hydra (*ch-ih*), which has the bearded head of a bird with a pointed beak, very similar to that of the phenix. The left hind foot of the monster terminates in a bird's head, presumably symbolizing a cloud. It is rearing the left fore paw in the direction of the bird, supporting the right on the clouds below." Dr. Laufer supposes that this design (which is very like those of the Shantung slabs mentioned above) signifies that the dragon is assisted by birds in moving clouds and in sending down rain; and he mentions that when rain is to be expected dragons

JADE PILGRIM BOTTLES WITH CARVED DRAGONS AND SACRED PEARL.
Chinese, eighteenth century. Courtesy of the Metropolitan Museum.

scream. "The dragon," Dr. Laufer continues, "in intimate connection with the growth of vegetation, appears as a deity . . . invoked in times of drouth with prayers for rain." The dictionary *Shuo Wen,* referring to a certain jade carving named 'lung,' placed on an altar as a prayer for rain, has the form and voice of a dragon. These Han jades were ring-shaped, but were soon superseded by engraved prayer-tablets. The Son of Heaven wore a robe embroidered with royal dragons when he sacrificed in the ancestral temple; his own memorial altar will have the dragon-tablet when he "has ascended upon the dragon to be a guest on high."

The dragon possesses the power of self-transformation, may make itself dark or luminous, or render itself invisible. A Chinese informed Mr. Ball that it becomes at will reduced to the size of a silkworm, or swollen till it fills the space of heaven and earth. When its breath escapes it forms clouds, sometimes changing into rain at other times into fire; and its voice is like the jingling of copper coins. Formerly, glass was thought to be its solidified breath. The creature may descend into the depths of the ocean, and rest in palaces of pearl.

In early days, if ancient books are trustworthy, there were tame dragons—they dragged the chariots of legendary kings; and Visser found a tradition of a family making it their business to breed them for the emperors—hence their family name Hwan-lung, 'dragon-rearer.' Later it became the custom to ornament the prows of pleasure-junks with dragon-heads, and certain kinds of long, slender boats are known as 'dragon-boats' to this day. A popular story relates the adventures of a sort of celestial Robin Hood, Feng Afoo-chow, who stole from the rich and gave to the poor. He rode about the country on a winged, fire-breathing dragon (precurser of the automobile?), righted wrongs and appropriated treasure, until at last he per-petrated a theft of such magnificence that he left it to be the crown of his career, and settled down to remain a law-abiding citizen until his tame dragon bore him to the heaven of the repentant rich.

The popular understanding is that dragons were supernatu-rally created but are of different sexes, and are able to repro-duce their kind; and according to Visser the book *Pei Ya* sup-ports the general opinion that they are born from eggs. When these are about to hatch the sound made by a male embryo makes the wind rise, whereas the cry of a female 'chick' causes the wind to abate and change its direction. One account of how the sexes differ explains that the male dragon's horn is "undulating, concave and steep"; it is strong on the top but very thin below. The female has a straight snout, a round mane, thin scales and a stout tail.

Dragons' eggs are the beautiful pebbles picked up beside mountain brooks; and they are preserved by nature until they split in a thunderstorm, releasing a young dragon which imme-diately goes up to the sky. An old woman who found such eggs had various adventures with them that children like to hear about. A dragon's egg much bigger than a hen's egg, light and apparently hollow, was found, history says, in the Great River in the tenth century; and to it, in the opinion of the local people, was due subsequent calamitous floods. An-other egg found was very heavy, and when shaken rattled as if it contained water; perhaps it was a geode—at any rate it became an object of worship.

An interesting legend is appropriate here. The uppermost and worst cataract in the Yangtse gorges, known as the New or Glorious Rapid, was formed in 1896 by a landslip that filled three-fourths of the channel. The rivermen account for this mishap thus, as related by Dingle: [14] "The ova of a dragon being deposited in the bowels of the earth at this particular spot in due course of time hatched out. . . . The baby dragon grew and grew, but remained in a dormant state until quite full-grown, when, as the habit of the dragon is, it became active, and at the first awakening shook down the hillside by a mighty effort, freed itself from the bowels of the earth, and made its way down to the sea."

A ford in the upper Hoang Ho is called Dragon-Gate. Fishes that pass above it become 'dragons'; those that fail remain simple fishes. Rapids and waterfalls in various parts of the country, and in Japan, have the same name and frequently a similar story.

Chapter Six

THE DRAGON AS A RAIN-GOD

I HAVE been speaking thus far of the Oriental dragon in a generic sense, trying to show the nature of a mythical, half-animal, semi-divine, wholly imaginary being, vague and intangible, swayed by human motives and emotions yet endowed with a demonic combination of ability and instability—a Chinese abstraction derived from a prehistorically antique awe of the serpent and clothed in the mystery of such a lineage; and most appropriate is it that such a quasi-deity should be worshipped at ancestral altars, for doubtless it is a relic of tribal, perhaps totemic, idolatry, an elaborate product of a long-forgotten animism.

"It is in China," wrote John Leyland a few years ago (*Magazine of Art,* Volume 14) "that the dragon reaches its highest pinnacle as an object of reverence . . . for it is markedly an object of propitiation, and festivals are held in its honour. Yet its connection with the root-ideas of the Hindoos is never lost, for it is a monster of mists and waters, and is painted issuing from clouds. . . . There is evidence also of human sacrifice to the monster, for Hieun Tsang relates that one Wat-Youen, on the failure of a river, immolated himself in propitiation of the dragon; and at the dragon-boat festivals it is now believed that the boats intimidate the monster. Such ideas were probably carried to China and Japan with Buddhism, for Buddha himself was a dragon-slayer—a destroyer of savage demonism and cruel magic."

The dragon of recent art, say since the time of the Mings, has lost, however, in the process of conventionalization, some of the characteristics that are needful to its complete composition, according to what may be designated as an official formula

A TYPICAL CHINESE DRAGON SEEN AMONG CLOUDS.

for making a perfect image of it. This is given by Joly [15] as follows:

"The Chinese call the dragon 'lung' because it is deaf. It is the largest of scaly animals, and it has nine characteristics. Its head is like a camel's, its horns like a deer's, its eyes like a hare's, its ears like a bull's, its neck like an iguana's, its scales like those of a carp, its paws like a tiger's, and its claws like an eagle's. It has nine times nine scales, it being the extreme of a lucky number. On each side of its mouth are whiskers,

75

under its chin a bright pearl, on the top of its head the 'poh shan' or foot-rule, without which it cannot ascend to heaven. The scales of its throat are reversed. Its breath changes into clouds from which come either fire or rain. The dragon is fond of the flesh of sparrows and swallows, it dreads the centipede and silk dyed of five colours. It is also afraid of iron. In front of its horns it carries a pearl of bluish colour striated with more or less symbolical lines."

Most of these features have been discussed elsewhere. The horns in many existing figures show plainly as two straight, smooth, level spikes from the back of the head, usually with one or more short, deer-like prongs and have no resemblance to the unbranched, curved, rugose horns of an antelope or goat; hence they do not suggest descent from those of the Babylonian 'goat-fish.' The scales, however, are regarded as piscine rather than ophidian; they seem to be related to those of the carp, with which the dragon in one of its aspects is closely connected. These scales, we learn, are properly eighty-one in number, that is nine times nine, which in mystical calculations represent *yang,* as the number six equals *yin.* Both golden and silver scales are spoken of in the Classics. The annals of Weihaiwei, studied by R. F. Johnston, contain a story on this point. "In the year 1732 there was a very heavy shower of rain [in Shantung]. In the sky, among the dark clouds, was espied a dragon. When the storm passed off a man named Chiang of the village of Ho Ch'ing or Huo Ch'ien picked up a thing that was as large as a sieve, round as the sun, thick as a coin, and lustrous as the finest jade. It reflected the sun's light and shone like a star, so that it dazzled the eyes. . . . The village soothsayer was appealed to for a decision. A single glance at the strange object was enough for the man of wisdom. 'This thing,' he said, 'is a scale that has fallen from the body of the dragon.' "

Chinese mythology and custom recognize (or used to) various separate kinds of dragons, species of the genus *lung*. The most ancient and highly respected of these are three: the *Lung* in the sky; the *Li* in the sea; and the *Kiau* in the marshes.

The first of this trio is properly styled *t'ien lung*, Celestial or Heavenly Dragon. It doubtless typifies and embodies the original object of veneration, and remains supreme and most sacred. It resides in the sky where it guards the mansions of the gods and sustains their power; as these powers are represented on earth by the sovereignty of the realm in the person of the emperor, it alone has the right to be attached to him and his affairs, and in that relation is designated Imperial Dragon. Hence it has long been recognized as the emblem of the Chinese empire, and was borne on its triangular flag and other appurtenances of government until the establishment of the present Republic; and it has well been remarked that nothing could express more forcibly the change of mind that has come over official China than the abandonment of this antique and venerated symbol.

The dragon in relation to the social constitution of the Chinese State falls into several classes or ranks, distinguished by the number of its claws. Thus representations of the imperial dragons proper, restricted to the emperor himself, should alone have five claws, while princes and nobles of lesser rank must be content with a less number. This sumptuary rule seems not to have been observed uniformly. We are told that on early coins and standards four-clawed dragons appeared as driven by prehistoric emperors. Chester Holcomb states in his

Catalogue that the imperial badge used during the Sung (tenth century A.D.) and previous dynasties was represented with three claws only; during the subsequent Ming period by four; and only during the most recent (Ching) period by five claws. Mr. Ripley insists, on the contrary, that the five-clawed form was introduced by the Ming rulers, as he thinks is proved by the carving on tombs of the early Ming emperors at Mukden. J. F. Blacker [16] gives the rule and practice in recent times thus: "The Imperial dragon is armed with five claws on each of its four members, and is used as an emblem by the emperor's family and by princes of the highest two ranks. The four-clawed dragon is used by princes of the third or fourth class. Mandarins and princes of the fifth rank have as an emblem the four-clawed serpent. The three-clawed dragon—the Imperial dragon of Japan—is in China the one commonly used for decoration." According to Albert J. Jacquemart, the mandarin four-clawed dragon became the conventionalized figure called *mang;* yet, despite their inferior rank, mangs adorn "many very superior articles of pottery and porcelain."

It appears, however, that it was not until the advent of the powerful and progressive Han dynasty began its enlightening and stimulating rule that dragons in various forms began to serve decorators. At first they seem to have been applied almost exclusively to royal robes and furnishings, but their use gradually broadened. Here first appeared winged dragons, the bird-like wings drawn indicating that the creature was to be regarded as a spring animal. Since that time, however, winged dragons have almost disappeared from both Chinese and Japanese art, as 'old-fashioned.' (In medieval Europe they were common, but the wings were more like those of bats.)

The second of the three 'great' dragons is the *shen-lung,* or

CHINESE HOLY MEN TRAVELLING TO THE BUDDHIST HEAVEN.
Chinese, eleventh century. Courtesy of the Metropolitan Museum.

'spiritual' species, which may be called that of the common people, for it is the one that wafts the rain-cloud and sprinkles the farmers' fields. Hence its image decorates household altars and is worshipped, especially when prolonged drouth threatens loss of expected crops.

It is in this matter of prayers for rain that the people of China nowadays regard the dragon as divine—it is beyond all else a rain-god. In his philosophical treatise *Kwan Tse,* one of the early Classics, Kwang Chung declares a dragon to be a god (*shen*) because in the water he covers himself with five colours, "that is, with the cardinal virtues," and can change his shape to go where he pleases under or above the earth. "He whose transformations are not limited by days, and whose ascending and descending are not limited by time, is called a god (*shen*)." Another ancient sage asserts the yellow dragon to be the quintessence of *shen* as it exerts the most power and is of the highest rank, therefore it is called 'imperial.' Laufer considers the dragon the embodiment of the fertilizing power of water and a veritable deity when invoked for rain, and he thinks that if we look on it as a deity "we shall arrive at a better understanding of the various conceptions of the dragon in religion and art: the manifold types and variations of dragons met with in ancient Chinese art are representations of different forces of nature, or are, in other words, different deities."

I was long puzzled to account for the close connection that seems to exist between the doctrines and practice of worshipping ancestors and that directed toward the dragon as the controller of rainfall and of its often destructive concomitant, the lightning. Why were these religious notions so closely interrelated? The totemic theory is unsatisfactory; and I will con-

fess that my cogitations were unproductive until I read a remarkable paper on serpent-worship by C. S. Wake,[17] from which
I will cite a paragraph that seems to give an enlightening explanation of the connection referred to:

The serpent-superstition is intimately connected [in China]
with ancestor-worship, probably originating among uncultured
tribes who, struck by the noiseless movement and the activity
of the serpent, combined with its peculiar gaze and marvellous
power of fascination, viewed it as a spirit-embodiment. As
such it would appear to have the superior wisdom and power
ascribed to the denizens of the spirit-world, and from this would
originate also the ascription to it of the power over life and
health, and over the moisture on which these benefits are de-
pendent. Among ancestor-worshipping peoples, however, the
serpent would be viewed as a good being who busied himself
about the interests of the tribe to which he had once belonged.
When the simple idea of a spirit-ancestor was transformed into
that of a Great Spirit, the father of the race, the attributes of
the serpent would be enlarged. The common ancestor would
be relegated to the heavens, and that which was necessary to
the life and well-being of his people would be supposed to be
under his care. Hence the Great Serpent was thought to have
power over the rains and the hurricane, with the latter of which
it was probably often identified.

A writer of the second century before Christ, says Visser,
explains that "clouds follow the dragon, winds follow the
tiger." These cloud-dragons are invited to dispense rain by
means of their likenesses, "wherefore when earthen [clay-made]
dragons are set up, *yin* and *yang* follow their likenesses and
clouds and rain arise." The making of such earthen images

is of forgotten antiquity. Rules existed for moulding and ornamenting them according to varying circumstances, and an elaborate ritual and set of costumes was long ago prescribed for the priests and officials in the praying for rain. The dragon-boats, to be described, had the same character and purpose. These ceremonies may be described as sympathetic magic intended to force the dragons to follow their images and to ascend from their pools to the skies; but often scolding and even flogging of the images has been necessary to bring about the desired action.

Dr. Visser found in a well-known old book, the *Wah Tsah Tsu*, dated near the end of the sixteenth century, information as to the significance of several different young dragons, whose shapes are used as ornaments, each according to its nature. Those that like to cry are represented on the tops of handles of bells; those that like music figure on musical instruments, and so forth. "The *ch'i-wen*, which like swallowing, are placed on both ends of the ridgepoles of roofs (to swallow all evil influences). The *chao-fung*, lion-like beasts which like precipices, are placed on the four corners of roofs." Sword-belts have as ornaments the murderous *ai-hwa*, and so on through a list of significant applications. Dragons are embroidered on the front curtains of catafalques and on grave-clothes, surrounded by many emblematic animals. It is not plain, however, that all these belong to the *shen* class. Laufer also mentions, in his paper on grave-sculptures, that in certain Han bas-reliefs on stone, dragons are "fettered by bands, i.e., do not send rain—are in a state of repose." These are surrounded by bird-shaped clouds which he interprets as tranquil clouds yielding no rain.

Whether the metaphysics of this matter of the relation between dragons and rainfall is comprehended by ordinary folk in the Flowery Kingdom may well be doubted; but at any rate when dry weather prevails too long clay images of the *shen-lung* are likely to be carried about the district, accompanied by priestly ceremonials and incantations arranged with carefully suitable accessories and colourings, the ritual and colours varying with the season of the year. This has been a custom since remote ages, but in modern times prayers inscribed on tablets of jade and metal are much used, or the appeal is made in a more public and forcible way than formerly by means of large, image-bearing processions. "The Chinese are adepts in the art of taking the Kingdom of Heaven by storm," remarks the author of *The Golden Bough!*

These great processions have been frequently described by travellers. Mr. Ball [17] says that in Canton, where he frequently witnessed them, the mock-rain-god is a serpentine creature of great girth and 150 to 200 feet long, made of lengths of gaily-coloured crêpe, and sparkling with tiny, spangle-like mirrors. "Every yard or so a couple of human feet—those of the bearers —buskined in gorgeous silk, are visible. The whole is fronted by an enormous head of ferocious aspect, before the gaping jaws of which a man manœuvres a large pearl, after which the dragon prances and wriggles." These figures are of two kinds (but on what ground is not stated by Mr. Ball), one sort having golden scales and the other silver scales. Such processions may occur whenever one seems called for, but are staged regularly about January 15 and June 5, dates representing the winter and summer solstices. The latter is the time of the dragon-boat festival; but before proceeding to that let me say that should no rain follow these ceremonial prayers the images are abused, even torn to pieces, to remind the god that he must do his duty or he will be similarly punished; furthermore he must do it properly and be watchful to stop the downpour when enough has fallen, or take the consequences. The story goes that once when the *lung* neglected to stop an immoderate storm the local mandarins put his image in jail, whereupon the downpour quickly ceased.

The famous Dragon-boat Festival of southern China is held on the fifth day of the fifth moon, which usually falls in our June. Tradition informs us that it began in commemoration of a virtuous minister of state, Chii Yuan, whose remonstrances against the unworthy acts of his sovereign were met by his dismissal and degradation. This happened some 450 years before Christ. He committed suicide, presumably by drowning, for on the first anniversary of his death began a search for his body in the water, which still continues in the form and meaning of this festival. More scientifically minded persons, however, such as Visser, De Groot, and Frazer, scout the pious tale, and regard this water-festival as in its origin an effort or supplication for rain. That it has become a time of feasting, fun and goodwill is doubtless owing to the sense of midsummer, celebrated by rejoicing in all parts of the world. In Burma and Siam, also, it is marked by three days of jollity when everybody plays with water, rowing, swimming, ducking one another, spraying the crowds in the streets from big syringes, and rollicking generally.

The principal feature in Southern China is a great number of boats and boat-races on the nearest river, with every gay and amusing accessory that can be devised. The boats used are built for the purpose, and are from 50 to 100 feet long, but only just wide enough for two men to sit abreast—that is, as near like water-snakes as is feasible. They are propelled as rapidly as possible—a traditional requirement—and the rowers try to keep time with the drums and gongs with which each one is provided. Impromptu races are challenged, often resulting in accidents, as the boats are slight, and dangerous when paddled by perhaps a hundred Chinamen wild with enthusiasm and unsteady with liquor. Large crowds of spectators occupy the river-banks urging their favourite boats to win, and the excitement and fun are intense.

The third member of the first class of dragons is *Li-lung* to whom belongs the earth and its waters, who marks out the courses of rivers and who is the ruler of the ocean. When a waterspout is seen the people view it reverently, saying: "Li is going up to heaven." This dragon is described as yellow, and as having a lion's body with a human-faced, hornless, dragon's head. The monster's quadrupedal form and close relation to sea and inland waters, indicate perhaps that it was introduced to the people of the southern and eastern coasts by early voyagers from the west bringing stories of Babylonian Ea and Marduk, and their sea-goat; so that it may really be a different species of partly separate origin from those of the western and northern interior.

As the earth-dragon, *Li* is supposed to exist beneath the surface, and to cause earthquakes by uneasy movements of its gigantic frame; and in one case, as has been noted, these movements, the boatmen say, caused a great landslide, which partly dammed the Yangtse and formed the dread rapids in the gorge above Ichang, called the Dragon's Gate. The fossil bones of huge reptiles—of which I shall have more to say presently—occasionally exhumed in various parts of China are thought by the people to be its bones, attesting to its prodigious size; and these bones are naturally endowed with magically curative qualities, as we shall see. This subterranean dragon is reputed to guard heaps of gold and silver and gems, and it is the protector of the veins of precious minerals in the underlying rocks.

It should be needless for me to say that no real animal of the more or less distant past was the ancestor or originator of the object of our study; yet I find this belief still held, vaguely, by even the most intelligent among my neighbours. Every fossil that has come to light, and formerly misled ignorant or unthinking men into supposing it a relic of a real ancestor, was buried and petrified millions of years before any human eyes to see, or minds to consider, it were in existence. The dragon is a pure figment of the human imagination.

As an oceanic divinity Li is believed to possess a great treasury under the sea in which he stores the wealth that comes to him from wrecked junks. Among his most precious possessions are the eyes of certain large fish, believed to be priceless gems; that is the reason, say the fisher-folk of Shantung, why big dead fish cast on the beaches are always eyeless— Lung Wang has added them to his hoard. So says St. Johnston,[5] and then tells us that in the Jung-ch'eng district is a pool of water which, though several miles in the interior from the Shantung coast, is said to taste of sea-salt, to be fathomless, and to remain always at sea-level; it is dedicated to the sea-dragon, locally known as *Lung Wang.* "One day an inquisitive villager tried to fathom its gloomy depths with his carrying-pole. Hardly had he immersed it in water when it was grasped by a mysterious force and wrenched out of his hand. It was immediately drawn below, and after waiting for its reappearance the villager went home. A few days later he was on the seacoast, gathering seaweed for roof-thatch, when suddenly he beheld his *pien-tang* floating in the water below the

85

rocks on which he was standing. On the first available opportunity after this he burned three sticks of incense in Lung-Wang's temple, as an offering to the deity that had given him so striking a demonstration of its miraculous power."

This one may be the "coiled dragon" (*Pan Lung*) mentioned by some writers, which "hibernates in the watery depths and marshes, and is often met with in the form of medallions in porcelain bowls and dishes." It may also be the creature referred to in a little story by L. J'. Vance (*Open Court*, 1892) of a small girl that fell into a Chinese river where boats and boatmen were numerous. "Nobody helped her, and when finally she caught at a rope and climbed on a boat, she was scolded, sent home and punished." The apathy exhibited was due to the belief that the river-dragon wanted that child and mysteriously caused her to fall overboard.

The account of the Golden Dragon Kings given by Dr. Du Bose [18] perhaps belongs here. These 'kings' are said to be yellow (?) snakes that come floating down the Hoang Ho in times of great flood. One of them is recognized by the priestly authorities as the 'golden dragon.' It has a square head with horns, and is hailed with delight as it signifies that the waters are about to recede. "The governor," Du Bose tells us without geographical particulars, "receives the divine snake in a lacquered waiter, carries him in his sedan to the temple, and the mandarins all worship the heaven-sent messenger. Many courtesies are offered him until at last he takes his leave. . . . Mandarins who do not believe in idolatry are entirely satisfied with the divinity of this snake."

One phase, or avatar, of this dragon seems to be that named *Yu Lung*, the special model and emblem of perseverance and success to literary aspirants who are seeking public offices by way of the stipulated education in the Classics—the only way in old times. This is the 'fish-dragon' so well illustrated on blue-and-white commercial jars, where the metamorphosis that links together the dragon and carp is variously depicted. The legend is that when a carp has succeeded in climbing over the cataracts in the Dragon Gate of the Yangtse it finds its reward by being transformed into a dragon, with which goes a grant of immortality. Seizing on the apt imagery of this legend, the fish-dragon was adopted as their 'patron-saint' by the students who toiled in their cheerless cells over the still more cheerless lore of long-dead sages, whose star of hope was the prospect of a government office and a possible chance for immortal fame, if only they could surmount the rocky obstacle of the official examinations. The parallel is grimly humorous! But cells, and classics and students are gone—and perhaps their patron-saint must go too.

Chapter Seven

KOREAN WATER AND MOUNTAIN SPIRITS

KOREA CAME very early in Oriental history under the influence, if not under the domination, of China, and a cult of the Dragon has existed there since antiquity. Dr. William E. Griffis,[19] in his valuable book *Corea, the Hermit Nation,* has this to say of its presence there under the local name *riong;* and some absurdly extravagant legends might be quoted.

"The riong [Li Lung?]," Dr. Griffis writes, "is one of the four supernatural or spiritually endowed creatures. He is an embodiment of all the forces of motion, change, and power for offence and defence in animal life, with the mysterious attributes of the serpent. There are many varieties of the genus Dragon. . . . In the spring it ascends to the skies, and in the autumn buries itself in the watery depths. It is this terrific manifestation of movement and power which the Corean artist loves to depict—always in connection with waters, clouds, or the sacred jewel of which it is the guardian."

There is also a terrestrial dragon, which presides over mines and gems; and the intense regard for it is perhaps the chief reason why mines have been so little worked in Chosen, the people superstitiously fearing that disasters may follow disturbance of the metals which they believe are peculiarly the treasure of this jealous earth-spirit.

"All mountains are personified in Korea," we are told by

DRAGON DESIGNS IN EMBROIDERY.

Japanese-Chinese, early eighteenth century. Courtesy
of the Metropolitan Museum.

Angus Hamilton,[20] and are "usually associated with dragons.
. . . In lakes there are dragons and lesser monsters. . . . The
serpent is almost synonymous with the dragon. Certain fish
in time become fish-dragons; snakes become elevated to the
dignity and imbued with the ferocity of dragons when they
have spent a thousand years in the captivity of the mountains
and a thousand years in the water. All these apparitions may
be propitiated with sacrifices and prayers."

The most important of Korean heights are the Diamond
Mountains, where the mines of the country are most extensively
worked, to the trepidation of the populace who anticipate that
some day a dreadful retribution will fall on the impious foreign exploiters of their mineral veins. "One dizzy height is
named Yellow Dragon, a second the Flying Phenix; and a
third, the Hidden Dragon, has reference to a demon who has
not yet risen from the earth upon his ascent to the clouds."

Mr. Hamilton gives a description of the temples of Yu-
chom-sa in the Diamond Mountains. Of one of them he says:
"The altar of this temple is adorned by a singular piece of
wood-carving. Upon the roots of an upturned tree sit or stand
fifty-three diminutive figures of Buddha. The monks tell an
old-world legend of this strange structure. Many centuries ago
fifty-three priests, who had journeyed from far India to Korea
to introduce the precepts of Buddha into this ancient land, sat
down by a well beneath a spreading tree. Three dragons presently emerged from the depths of the well and attacked the
fifty-three, calling to their aid the wind dragon, who thereupon uprooted the tree. As the fight proceeded the priests
managed to place an image of Buddha on each root of the
tree, converting the whole into an altar, under whose influence
the dragons were forced back into their cavernous depths, when

huge rocks were piled into the well to shut them up. The monks then founded the monastery, building the main temple above the remains of the vanquished dragons."

Apart from any historical suggestions which this interesting story may contain, one notes that the exorcism of the threatening demons was accomplished in just the same way as Christian monks did by a show of the Cross, as we shall see when we come to consider the dragon-lore of mediæval Europe.

Whatever is most excellent the Koreans compare to the divinely virtuous Dragon. A 'dragon-child' is one that is a paragon of propriety; 'a dragon-horse,' one having great speed, and so on to indicate the superlative. A common proverb, "When the fish has been transformed into the dragon," means that a happy change has taken place. This embodiment of good nature and good luck is, of course, simply the Chinese *lung,* friendly and worthy of respect and worship.

It appears, however, that Buddhistic travellers and missionaries from cobra-worshipping India, corrupted this gentle faith long ago by the introduction of the Hindoo doctrines and practice of naga-worship, inculcating a system of diabolism that filled the land with fear and defensive magic: the cheerful old dragons of the past became horrid snakes, lurking in every pool, and filling the seas with terror. A Korean book describes an exorcist of nagas who went with his pitcher full of water to the pond inhabited by a naga, and by his magic formulæ surrounded the reptile with a ring of fire. As the water in the pitcher was its only refuge the naga turned himself into a small snake and crept into the pitcher. Whether the exorcist then killed him the story does not reveal; but in the tale Visser finds evidence of the nagas "not only as rain-gods, but also as beings wholly dependent on the presence of water and much afraid of fire—just like the dragons in Chinese and Japanese legends."

Hulbert,[21] author of *The Passing of Korea,* describes things and ideas as they were before the modernization of the country by the Japanese. He informs us that every Korean river and stream, as well as the surrounding oceans, was formerly believed to be the abode of a dragon, and every village on the banks of a stream used to make periodic adoration to this power. The importance of paying so much formal respect to it lay in the fact that this aquatic dragon had control of the rainfall, and had to be kept in good humour lest the crops be endangered by insufficient showers; furthermore it was able to make great trouble for boatmen and deep-sea sailors unless properly appeased. Hence not only the villagers and farmers, but the owners and masters of ships desiring favourable weather for their voyaging, made propitiatory sacrifices—not alone the important war-junks, but the freight-boats, fishermen, ferry-boats, etc., each conducting its own kind of ceremony to ensure safety. In all cases it was addressed as tribute to a water-spirit.

The ceremony, at least when held on land, was performed by a *mudang* (a professional female exorcist) in a boat, accompanied by as many of the leading persons of the village as were able to crowd in with her. "Her fee is about forty dollars. The most interesting part of the ceremony is the mudang's dance, which is performed on the edge of a knife-blade laid across the mouth of a jar that is filled to the brim with water." Even more elaborately nonsensical was the ceremony on a ferryboat—a great institution in a land without bridges, as Korea used to be.

Mr. Hulbert says that not until the beginning of the reign

of the present dynasty was the horrible custom of throwing a young virgin into the sea at Py-ryung, as a propitiatory offering to the demon of the ocean-world, discontinued. "At that place the mudang held an annual *séance* in order to propitiate the sea-dragon and secure plenteous rains for the rice-crop and successful voyages for the mariners." With the change of the royal house a new prefect was appointed to the district, who had no faith or sympathy with either the theory or its frightful demands. He attended the next *séance,* where he found three mudangs dragging a screaming girl towards the seashore. Stopping them he asked whether it was really necessary that a human being be sacrificed. They answered that it was. "Very well," he said; "*you* will do as an offering." Signing to two policemen they tied and hurled one of the mudangs into the waves. The dragon gave no sign of displeasure, and a second, and after her the third, were 'sacrificed' without any visible response from the demon the people had been taught to fear. This demonstration ended the practice and the profession of the mudangs together.

Chapter Eight

"THE MEN OF THE DRAGON BONES"

WHEN IN September, 1923, Dr. Henry Fairfield Osborn, President of the American Museum of Natural History in New York, was on his way to visit the camps of the Third Asiatic Exploring Expedition, conducted by Dr. Roy Chapman Andrews, aided by a staff of expert assistants, he halted for the night at a frontier Chinese village. Strolling about the station in the early evening, as he relates in the Museum's magazine *Natural History* (May-June, 1924):

I suddenly noticed a small group of men in the darkness pointing toward Andrews and myself. I asked Andrews to listen to what they were saying, and it was here that I learned the Chinese designation of our party, for the words were:
"There go the American men of the dragon bones!"
I was delighted with this Chinese christening, because it seemed to me both a tribute to the valour of our men and a wonderfully apt designation of the main objective of the Third Asiatic Expedition as it impressed itself upon the Chinese. For what purpose were we in Mongolia? Obviously enough to the Chinese mind to collect the bones of dragons—the dragons which for ages past had ruled the sky, the air, the earth, the waters of the earth, and which even today are believed in implicitly by the Chinese. Of course we should find small bones

93

corresponding to small dragons, large bones corresponding to remains of large dragons—also of vast dragons, some of which, according to Chinese myth, leave their tails in the eastern part of the desert of Gobi while their heads rest on the slopes of the Altai Mountains, four hundred miles distant!

Here is the sum of the paleontology and zoology of the native Chinese—the dragon and the phenix.

The 'dragon bones' were the fossilized remains of prehistoric animals for which the men of science were searching the deserts of Mongolia, the discovery of which, then and since, have added vastly to the sum of paleontology and increased the world's knowledge of and interest in China and Central Asia, and in their inhabitants and history. Incidentally these explorations have illuminated certain obscurities in the broad and antique myth now engaging the reader's attention.

Fossil bones have long been known to the Chinese, although almost nobody, even the wisest, had any just notion of the sort of creatures they represented. One may find in every apothecary's shop their fragments, or the powder made by crushing them, but rarely can a druggist tell you whence they came, for the wholesale dealers are loath to reveal trade-secrets. They offer them as the bones of dragons which, when properly administered, must have strong curative virtues; the source of supply is, in their view, unimportant either for trade or healing —the more mystery about it the better. As everybody believes this, not suspecting any magic in the matter, the demand is so extensive that an immense supply of bones is annually gathered and dispensed.

Various theories exist among the people, however, as to the nature of these bones. It was generally agreed in the past that they were the cast-off skeletons of living dragons which had sloughed away their bones as well as their hides—once in a thousand years according to one authority; but some persons, with less credulity even in those ancient days, pronounced them the bones of dead dragons. This was much nearer the truth, for we now know that they are the fossilized skulls and limbs of real animals of long-past eras; and in our own time it has been soberly argued that from these fossils has been built up the whole fabric of faith in the reality of dragons past and present.

From this universal faith has arisen the popular trust in the therapeutic value of these mid-Tertiary fossils. According to the *Pen-ts'ao Kang-Muh*, the best source of information as to medical practice among the ancients, and extensively quoted by Visser, from whom I borrow again, the best bones are those having five colours, corresponding to the five visceral parts of the human body, namely: liver, lungs, heart, kidneys and spleen. White and yellow specimens rank next in healing value, and black ones are poorest, while those gathered by women are useless. Thin, broad-veined bones are regarded as female; those coarse and with narrow veins as male.

The preparation of the bones for administration in medicine is described as follows by Lei Hiao: "For using dragon's bones first cook odorous plants; bathe the bones twice in hot water; pound them to powder, and put this in bags of gauze. Take a couple of young swallows, and after having taken out their intestines and stomach, put the bags in the swallows and hang them over a well. After one night take the bags out of the swallows, rub the powder, and mix it into medicines for strengthening the kidneys. The efficacy of such a medicine is as it were divine." An author of the Sung dynasty recommends that the bones are to be soaked in spirits for one night, then dried on the fire and rubbed to powder. Another authority warns the people that some bones are a little poisonous, and in preparing and using them iron instruments and utensils should be avoided, because, as is well known, dragons dislike iron.

The list of illnesses curable by means of dragon-bones is a long one. Their curative power is attributed to the strong *yang* virtue in the bone, which makes *yin* demons abandon those portions of the body in which they have been trying to establish themselves. The teeth and horns of dragons are especially good for diseases developing madness, or difficulty in breathing, or convulsions, also for liver diseases. A Sung physician explains that, because the dragon is the god of the Eastern Quarter, his bones, horns and teeth can conquer any disorganization of the liver.

A book of the ninth century carries the information that when dragon's blood enters the earth it becomes amber; and in the *Pen-ts'ao Kang-Muh* you may read: "Dragon saliva is seldom used as a medicine. . . . Last spring the saliva spit out by a herd of dragons appeared floating [on the sea]. The aborigines gathered, obtained and sold it, each time for 2000 copper coins." Another treatise, written in the Sung period, instructs us that the most precious of all perfumes is seadragon's spittle, which is hardened by the sun, floats, and is blown ashore by the wind in hard pieces. This may be amber, or ambergris. Another source of perfume is the froth produced by fighting dragons.

From the same book, says Visser, we learn that anciently, at least, dragons' blood, fat, brains, saliva, etc., were also deemed useful as medicines, but how obtained is not clear from the Classics. "Perfumes were made from the spit; hence it was asserted that fighting dragons might be smelt. An old emperor used dragon's spittle for ink for writing on jade and gold. Having got a quantity of saliva he mixed it with the fruit of a herb which bore flowers in all four seasons. This produced a red liquid which penetrated into gold and jade."

Many more particulars as to this medicinal use of the bones are given by H. N. Moseley in his book *Notes of a Naturalist on the Challenger.*

When, early in the present century, the Geological Survey of China was organized, little more was known of the geology of that country than its broad outlines. Well aware that thousands of fossil skeletons of the utmost importance to science were being ground to powder and swallowed by millions of people daily, it was plain that the discovery of the sources of supply would lead to the paleontological knowledge so much desired; but between general ignorance and the jealousy of wholesale collectors and merchants of the bones it was difficult to learn where the fossils were found. Therefore when, in 1921, Professor Osborn and Mr. Walter Granger sought to co-operate with the China Survey, all the Director of the Survey could say was that he had been told that at a place in eastern Szechuan a short distance above I-chang, on the Yangtse River, many fossils had been excavated for the medicine dealers. Mr. Granger went there and finally learned that the spot was near a small village called Yin-ching-ao, twenty miles from the town of Wan Hsien, and there Granger made his residence. He described the situation in *Natural History,* for May-June, 1922, as follows:

The fossils at Yinchingkao occur in pits distributed along a great limestone ridge about thirty or forty miles in length and rising above our camp more than 200 feet. These pits are the result of the dissolving action of water on limestone, and some of them have a depth of one hundred feet or more. They are of varying sizes averaging say six feet in diameter, and are filled with a reddish and yellowish mud, which is, I take it, disintegrated limestone. The fossils are found imbedded in the mud at varying depths, usually below twenty feet. A crude windlass is rigged up over the pit, and the mud is dug out and hauled to the surface in scoop-shaped baskets. At fifty feet it is dark in the pit, and the work is done by the light of a tiny oil wick. . . . The excavation has been going on for a long time—possibly for several generations. Digging is done only in the winter months.

The excavation of the pits is opening up just now on a large scale, and in the coming month will probably give us about all we can take care of. The fauna is Stegodon, a primitive elephant, Bison, Bos, Cervus, Tapirus, Sus, Rhinoceros, besides many small ruminants, several carnivores, and many rodents; no horses, queerly enough.

The natives in taking out the bones used no care to preserve them whole; they knew they were destined to be pulverized for medicinal purpose, so why be careful. Each day's 'catch' was brought down to the village and piled up in a corner of the digger's house to await the coming of the buyers, who from time to time visited the village and collected the stock, paying about $20 a picul (133 lbs.). One can imagine the heartsick emotions of a paleontologist exploring an unknown fauna, as he viewed these local heaps of fragments of skulls and skeletons, or the many tons of them heaped in the warehouses at

I-chang—how he would pick out teeth and recognizable pieces and attempt to interpret them. By careful watching, instruction and rewards to the diggers, however, many skulls and other parts were procured uninjured, and so on this and subsequent visits a valuable collection was gradually accumulated, and divided between the museums in Peking and New York. As the report of such operations rapidly spread, it is not surprising that the wondering Chinese dubbed the American scientific staff "Men of the Dragon Bones."

Chapter Nine

THE DRAGON IN JAPANESE ART

"HAVE YOU seen the dragon?" asks Mr. Okakura in *The Awakening of Japan.* "Approach him cautiously, for no mortal can survive the sight of his entire body. The eastern dragon is not the gruesome monster of mediæval imagination, but the genius of strength and goodness. He is the spirit of change, therefore of life itself. . . . Hidden in the caverns of inaccessible mountains, or coiled in the unfathomed depths of the sea, he awaits the time when he slowly arouses himself into activity. He unfolds himself in the storm-clouds; he washes his mane in the blackness of the seething whirlpools. His claws are in the fork of the lightning, his scales begin to glisten in the bark of rain-swept pine-trees. His voice is heard in the hurricane, which, scattering the withered leaves of the forest, quickens a new spring. The dragon reveals himself only to vanish."

Joly continues these impressions thus: "The dragon is full of remarkable powers, and seeing its body in its entirety means instant death; the monster never strikes without provocation, as, for instance, when its throat is touched. The Chinese emperor Yao was said to be the son of a dragon, and several of the other Chinese rulers were metamorphically called 'dragon-faced.' The emperor of Japan was described in the same way, and as such [in old times was] hidden by means of bamboo curtains from the gaze of persons to whom he granted audiences to save them from a terrible fate.

Let me insert here two remarkable paragraphs from Dr. William E. Griffis's standard work on old Japan, say previous to fifty years ago:

Chief among ideal creatures in Japan is the dragon. The word 'dragon' stands for a genus of which there are several species and varieties. To describe them in full, and to recount minutely the ideas held by the Japanese rustics concerning them would be to compile an octavo work on dragonology. . . . In the carvings on tombs, temples, dwellings and shops—on the government documents—printed on the old and the new paper money, and stamped on the new coins—in pictures and books, on musical instruments, in high relief on bronzes, and cut in stone, metal and wood,—the dragon (tasu) everywhere "swinges the scaly horror of his folded tail," whisks his long moustaches, or glares with his terrible eyes. The dragon is the only animal in modern Japan that wears hairy ornaments on the upper lip. . . .

There are many kinds of dragons, such as the violet, the yellow, the green, the red, the white, the black and the flying-dragon. When the white dragon breathes, the breath of its lungs goes into the earth and turns to gold. When the violet dragon spits, the spittle becomes balls of pure crystal, of which gems and caskets are made. One kind of dragon has nine colours on its body, and another can see everything within a hundred ri; another has immense treasures of every sort; another delights to kill human beings. The water-dragon causes floods of rain; when it is sick the rain has a fishy smell. The fire-dragon is only seven feet long, but its body is of flame. The dragons are all very lustful, and approach beasts of every sort. The fruit of a union of one of these monsters with a

101

cow is the kirin; *with a swine, an elephant; and with a mare a steed of the finest breed. The female dragon produces at every parturition nine young. The first young dragon sings, and likes all harmonious sounds, hence the tops of Japanese bells are cast in the form of this dragon; the second delights in the sound of musical instruments, hence the* koto *or horizontal harp, and* suzumi, *a girl's drum, struck by the fingers, are ornamented with the figure of this dragon; the third is fond of drinking, and likes all stimulating liquors, therefore goblets, and drinking-cups are adorned with representations of this creature; the fourth likes steep and dangerous places, hence gables, towers, and projecting beams of temples and pagodas have carved images of this dragon upon them; the fifth is a great destroyer of living things, fond of killing and bloodshed, therefore swords are decorated with golden figures of this dragon; the sixth loves learning, and delights in literature, hence on the covers and titles of books and literary works are pictures of this creature; the seventh is renowned for its power of hearing; the eighth enjoys sitting, hence the easy chairs are carved in its images; the ninth loves to bear weight, therefore the feet of tables and* hibachi *are shaped like this creature's feet.*

Marcus Huish [22] gives a description of the figure that has become conventionalized among the artists of Japan in the following terms, which show that it differs markedly from the Chinese convention: "A composite monster with scowling head, long straight horns, a scaly, serpentine body, a *bristling row of dorsal spines,* four limbs armed with claws, and curious flamelike appendages on its shoulders and hips. The claws are usually three on each foot, but are sometimes four or even five." A famous print by Ichiyusai Hiroshige shows a dragon in a cloud about Fuji, which has three bird-like toes and claws on every foot.

I have underscored the item of the row of spines along the ridge of the back, for that is a special characteristic (sometimes a double row, as in those turned about the bronze drum at Nara), and significant in relation to its history; and in general its figure is more distinctly that of a serpent than is the typical dragon of China. Its name in Japanese is *Tatsu,* the equivalent of the Chinese *Lung;* and in both countries it serves as one of the signs of the zodiac in the place occupied by Leo in the European symbols of the sun's stations in its apparent annual circuit of the heavens. It also represents the four seas which, as in the Chinese cosmogony, limit the habitable earth, and are ruled by four dragon kings. "The snake," says G. E. Smith, "takes a more obtrusive part in the Japanese than in the Chinese dragon, and it frequently manifests itself as a god of the sea. The old Japanese sea-gods were often female water-snakes. The cultural influences which reached Japan from the south by way of Indonesia—many centuries before the coming of Buddhism—naturally emphasized the serpent form of the dragon and its connection with the ocean. But the river-gods, or 'water fathers,' were real four-footed dragons identified with the dragon-kings of Chinese myth, but at the same time were strictly homologous with the naga-rajas or cobra-kings of India."

Joly describes the four 'dragon kings' recognized in Japan as follows:

Sui Riu—*a rain-dragon, which when in pain causes reddish rain, coloured by its blood.*

Han-Riu—*striped with nine different colours; forty feet long; can never reach heaven.*

103

Ka Riu—*scarlet; fiery; only seven feet long.*
Ri Riu—*has wonderful sight; can see more than 100 miles.*
The dragon queen is occasionally shown in art dressed in shells, corals, and other marine attributes.

The Chinese winged dragon *ying lung* (rare in decorations) is the *hai riu* of the Japanese, and is shown with feathered wings, a bird's claws and tail, and a dragon's head; it is also called *tobi tatsu* and *sachi hoko*. Children are told of a dragon with a fish's body clothed in large scales; it is called *maketsugo*, and may be a nursery version of the Chinese carp-and-dragon story. The dragon of good luck is *fuku riu*, contrasted with which is one of bad luck. It is popularly believed that dragons may breed by intercourse with earthly animals as a cow or mare, and in folklore a special name is given to each kind of hybrid so resulting. Joly, whose interest in this subject is in explaining its symbolism in art, says that a dragon ascending Fuji in a cloud is symbolic of success in life; that one issuing from a hibachi has the proverbial significance of "It is the unexpected that happens"; and that in connection with a tiger, usually drawn near a cave or some bamboos, the dragon in the sky above represents the power of the elements over the strongest animals. (We have seen hitherto that the tiger is the antithesis of the dragon in many situations.) Joly concludes: "As an emblem the dragon represents both the male and female principles, the continual changes and variations of life, as symbolized by its unlimited powers of adaptation, accommodating itself to all surroundings."

A Japanese myth represents Susan-o-no-o-no Mikoto as an 'impetuous' man who killed an eight-headed dragon, or snake, by making the brute drunk with eight cups of sake (one for

JAPANESE CANDLESTICK WITH COILED DRAGON.
Courtesy of Mrs. Frances Buchanan Ingersoll.

each head)', and then cutting off all the heads at once. (Eight is a number of great significance in Buddhistic mysticism.) From the tail he drew a marvellous sword, later consecrated to and preserved in the temple of Atsuta. A sword got from a dragon figures, by the way, in several other legends; and various dragons are common ornaments of sword-guards and netsukes, presumably with symbolic intent.

Another version of this story runs thus: A man came to a house where all were weeping, and learned that the last of eight daughters of the house was to be given to a dragon with seven (?) or eight heads, which came to the seashore yearly to claim a victim. He changed himself into the form of the girl, and induced the dragon to drink sake from eight pots set before it, and then slew the drunken monster. From the end of its tail he took out a sword which is supposed to be the Mikado's state sword. The hero married the maid and with her got a jewel or talisman, which is preserved with the royal regalia. Another prize so preserved is a mirror.

Commenting on these tales from Japanese folklore, Dr. G. Elliot Smith[4] expresses the opinion that the appearance in them of a seven-headed monster adds to the probability of their importation from the West, and regards it as a reminiscence of the Egyptian Seven Hathors myth. "The seven-headed dragon is found also in the Scottish dragon-myth, and the legends of Cambodia, India, Persia, western Asia, East Africa, and the Mediterranean area. . . . In southern India the Dravidian people seem to have borrowed the Egyptian idea of the seven Hathors. . . . There is a close analogy between the Swahili and the Gaelic stories that reveals their ultimate derivation from Babylonia. In the Scottish story the seven-headed dragon comes in a storm of wind and spray. The East African serpent comes in a storm of wind and dust. In the Babylonian story seven winds destroy Tiamat. . . . But the Babylonians not only adopted the Egyptian conception of the power of evil as being seven demons, but they also seem to have fused these seven into one."

Foremost, however, among Japanese dragon-legends is that of Riujin and his submarine palace Ryugo-Jo. His messenger is Riuja (or Hakuja), a small white serpent with the face of an ancient man. To the anger of this dragon-king of the sea we owe the boisterous waves. Joly instructs us that he is usually represented by artists as a very old, long-bearded man with a dragon coiled on his head or back. Some say that a man named Hoori once visited the sea-god's palace and got a wife whom he brought ashore and married in earthly fashion; but as soon as the first baby came the wife became a dragon again and sank under the surface of the sea. Other tales are told of visits of this submarine ruler of storms, some of which deal with marvellous gems romantically recovered.

This brief sketch indicates that the dragon is a different affair in Japan from what it is in China, despite a superficial similarity. In both countries the learned and more or less modernized top-crust of society is, or pretends to be, unaffected by this superstition—if it be permissible so to designate it— but this unbelieving class is far broader and deeper in Japan than in China, although still finding in the dragon of tradition an art-motive which is more than merely effective in decoration, for it is instinct with an antique sentiment which all cannot help feeling. This sympathy and sense of symbolism, fostered by the romantic wonder-tales of childhood, in which the dragon figured, is perhaps stronger in sensitive Japan than among the more matter-of-fact Chinese; while faith in the actuality of dragons and the reality of their powers and divine influence is much stronger among the latter people than in Japan.

I shall quote here a paragraph illustrating this point from that most delightful book, John La Farge's *An Artist's Letters from Japan*. The author is speaking of what he saw at Nikko when visiting the splendid temple built by the Tokugawa rulers in memory of the great shogun Iyéyasu, who died in 1616, and was buried and deified on the Holy Mountain of Nikko. It is entered by the gate called 'magnificent,' above which is an ornate balcony.

The balcony is one long set of panels—of little panels carved and painted on its white line with children playing among flowers. Above, again, as many white pillars as below; along their sides a wild fringe of ramping dragons and the pointed leaves of the bamboo. This time the pillars are crowned with the fabulous dragon-horse, with gilded hoofs dropping into air, and lengthy processes of horns receding far back into the upper bracketings of the roof. Upon the centre of the white-and-gold lintel, so delicately carved with waves as to seem smooth in this delirium of sculpture, is stretched between two of the monster capitals a great white dragon with gilded claws and gigantic protruding head. But all these beasts are tame if compared with the wild army of dragons that cover and people the innumerable brackets which make the cornice and support the complicated rafters under the roof. Tier upon tier hang farther and farther out, like some great mass of vampires about to fall. They are gilded; their jaws are lacquered red far down into their throats, against which their white teeth glitter. Far into the shade spreads a nightmare of frowning eyebrows, and pointed fangs and outstretched claws

107

*extended toward the intruder. It would be terrible did not one
feel the coldness of the unbelieving imagination, which perhaps merely copied these duplicates of earlier terrors.*

An interesting legend, which has been made the theme of
a popular Japanese play, is related by Arthur D. Ficke in his
Catalogue of colour-prints, 1920. In the tenth century the
monk Anchin, having repulsed the amorous advances of an in-
fatuated girl Kiyohime, fled from her wrath and hid in the
shadows beneath the great bell that hung in the grounds of the
temple at Dojoji, in the Province of Kii, near Kyoto. She, having procured the aid of evil spirits, pursued him; and transforming herself into a dragon she touched the enormous bell,
which at once fell to the ground covering the unfortunate
priest. Thereupon the revenged dragon-woman curled her fiery
length about the bell and, lashing it into a white heat with her
flaming body, she consumed her reverent lover and perished
herself as the bell collapsed in a molten flood.

The prevalence of the Shinto doctrines in Japan has weak-
ened, no doubt, the more corrupt and superstitious features of
mediæval Buddhism, and the natural gentleness and sensitiveness to beauty in the Japanese have freed them from the gross-
ness and terror belonging to such ideas and rites as came with
the horrible naga-cult imparted to their ancestors by early travellers and emissaries from India. Relics of this ancient demonism remain, however, in both their literature and their antique
art. The emphasis put in the legends on the sea-god in his
submarine palace, and his attendants of both sexes, their ability
to become humanized and to mate on shore with human beings,
show distinctly an Indian origin.

Climate also has had an effect here as elsewhere on men's

views of life. The dragon in northern and central China, at least, is primarily a rain-god, as it was in Mesopotamia and in the valley of the Indus, where drouths were dreaded. In Japan, on the contrary, rain was rarely lacking in agriculture, so that prayers for it were seldom necessary—often, rather, were petitions that its excess should cease. Hence among landsmen the principal motive for prayer and sacrifice to sky-dragons, at any rate, disappeared; while the scarcity of dangerous snakes destroyed the fear of and consequent veneration for serpents, so that actual naga-worship probably never took a strong hold of the people. What held most firmly and longest was the notion of a sea-god, for the Japanese have ever been mariners, and all seamen are inclined to love mysteries and to deify the wondrous phenomena of the ocean.

Chapter Ten

THE DRAGON'S PRECIOUS PEARL

A MOST curious, interesting, and at the same time obscure feature of this whole baffling subject is that of the so-called Pearl which accompanies the dragon in pictures and legends from the earliest times, and is common to the religious traditions of the whole East—India, China and Japan. Necklaces of pearls are a regular part of the regalia of naga-queens in their submarine palaces; and we read often in the old Vedic books of a magical 'jewel of good luck,' which was in custody of the naga-maidens but was lost by them through terror of their monstrous enemy, the bird *garuda*. There are traces of it in early Taoism, but it is best preserved in Buddhism as the jewel in the lotus, the *mani* of the mystic, ecstatic, formula *Om mani padme hum*—the "jewel that grants all desires," the 'divine pearl' of the Buddhists throughout the Orient. Koreans commonly believe that the yellow (chief) dragon carries on his forehead (as also in Japan) a pear-shaped pearl having supernatural properties and healing power. In China alone, however, is this mystical accessory of the dragon made a significant part of pictures and decorative designs. Some say that originally every proper dragon carried a pearl under his chin; others that it was a special mark of imperial rank. A sixth-century writer asserts that such pearls are "spit out of dragons like snake-pearls out of snakes," and have enormous value.

This extraordinary gem is represented as a spherical object, or 'ball,' half as big, or quite as large, as the head of the dragon with which it is associated, for it is never depicted quite by itself. The gem is white or bluish with a reddish or golden halo, and usually has an antler-shaped 'flame' rising from its surface. Almost invariably there hangs downward from the centre of the sphere a dark-coloured, comma-like appendage, frequently branched, wavering below the periphery. A biologist might easily at first glance conclude that the whole affair represented the entry of a spermatozoon into an ovum; and the Chinese commonly interpret the ball with its comma-mark as a symbol of *yang* and *yin,* male and female elements, combined in the earth—which seems pretty close to the biologist's view. Such is the Dragon-Pearl.

In purely decorative work, where the figure of a dragon is writhing in clouds or adapting its lithe body under an artist's hand to the shape or purpose of a piece of porcelain, a bronze article, or a silken garment, the pearl may be drawn close to the dragon, or wherever convenient. When, however, it is desirable to express the significance of this sacred adjunct of dragonhood, it is treated with strict attention to reverence and tradition. Then are pictured celestial dragons ascending and descending through the upper air, tearing a path, perhaps, through swirling mists and shadows, "in pursuit of effulgent jewels or orbs that appear to be whirling in space, and that were supposed to be of magic efficiency, granting every wish." A passion for gems is a well-known characteristic of these beings, and that it has 'always' been so is shown by a fable recorded by Joly. T'an T'ai Mieh Ming, a disciple of Confucius, was attacked, at the instigation of the god of the Yellow River, by two dragons seeking to rob him of a valuable gem;

111

but T'an T'ai slew the dragons and then, to show his contempt for worldly goods, threw the treasure into the river. Twice it leaped back into his boat, but at last he broke it in pieces and scattered the fragments.

Can these be the two dragons so often depicted facing one another in the air, and apparently rushing, as if in eager play, toward a pearl floating like an iridescent bubble between them? Nothing in the decorative art of China has occasioned more guessing and controversy than this. An eighteenth century vase described by Chait is "decorated with nine dragons (a mystic number) whirling through scrolled clouds enveloping parts of their serpentine bodies in pursuit of jewels of omnipotence, which appear in the midst of clouds as revolving disks emitting branched rays of effulgence." Ball points out that in books issued under imperial auspices "two dragons encircle the title, striving . . . for a pearl." Japanese designers like to form the handles of bells, whether big temple-bells or tiny ones, of two dragons *affrontés*, with the *tama* between them. One Japanese carving represents a snake-like dragon coiled tightly around a ball, marked with spiral lines, illustrating devotion to the *tama*. "A great ball of gilded glass," writes Visser, "is said to hang from the centre of the roof of the great hall of the Buddhist temple Fa(h)-yu-sze, or Temple of the Reign of Law, while eight dragons, curved around the 'hanging pillars,' eagerly stretch their claws towards the 'pearl of perfection.' . . . Dragons trying to seize a fiery 'pearl,' which is hanging in a gate, are represented twice in the same temple. . . . We may be sure that the Chinese Buddhists, identifying the Dragon with the Naga, also identified the ball with their *cintamani* or 'precious pearl which grants all desires.' "

112

In these and many similar examples we, as outsiders, may grasp little of the significance or symbolism in this conspicuous 'ball' or 'pearl,' but we may approach an understanding of it through Dr. De Groot's investigation of Chinese religion.[9] He describes the ceremonial dress of the Wuist priests as having a "broad border of blue silk around the neck stitched with two ascending dragons which are belching out a ball probably representing thunder." De Groot explains further that "the ball between two dragons is often delineated as a spiral," and adds that 'in an ancient charm . . . a spiral denotes the rolling of thunder from which issues a flash of lightning." In Japanese prints a dragon is frequently accompanied by a huge spiral indicating a thunderstorm caused by him. Are the antler-shaped appendages rising above the 'ball' intended to represent lightning-flames?

Dr. Visser discusses this hypothesis at length, pointing out that the whole attitude of the two dragons in such art-productions displays great eagerness to catch and swallow the gleaming sphere. This attitude and avidity become clear, Visser thinks, when one sees a Chinese picture like that in Blacker's *Chats on Oriental China*, of two dragons rushing at a fiery spiral ball above the legend: "Two Dragons Facing the Moon." Sometimes two dragons confront each other, each having a flaming pearl floating just in front of their faces.

There is nothing absurd about this suggestion of swallowing the moon. Celestial dragons are, in reality, personifications of clouds; and among the most primitive and widespread impressions respecting lunar eclipses is the notion that a monster is devouring the moon. Dark and writhing clouds advancing as if alive, and finally extinguishing its light, might easily suggest a similar thought; and it was a matter of early experience that after these hungry cloud-dragons had completed their feast, fertilizing rain usually blessed the thirsty fields and pastures, so that the dragons got the credit. Hence artists liked to represent these public benefactors playfully contending for the opportunity to devour the 'queen of night' and so produce a crop-saving fall of showers for which they (the dragons) would enjoy grateful appreciation. Incidentally, artists note that a pair of their graceful figures make a well-balanced composition. The moon and water are closely connected in all mythologies; hence the moon is closely linked with fertilizing agencies in general. Faith in the moon's influence on the weather lingers strongly in the mind of rural communities even in these progressive United States of America; and it is easy to believe that the dragon-thanking agriculturists and shepherds of China felt assured that the rain-giving will and power of their celestial friends were refreshed by frequently absorbing this bright and stimulating object in the sky.

That these reflections are not 'all moonshine' is shown by evidence in the writings of the old philosophers of the East, who assure us that the actual mundane pearl taken from the oyster in whose shell it is formed beneath the salt waters is the "concrete essence of the moon" distilled through the system of the mollusk—an emanation from the moon-goddess herself. "The pearls found in the oyster," as one student interprets it, "were supposed to be little moons, drops of the moon-substance (or dew) which fell from the sky into the gaping oyster. Hence pearls acquired the reputation of shining by night, like to the moon from which they were believed to have come." All this tends to demonstrate that the theory that the moon is the *mani*, the 'pearl of great price,' the divine essence of the gods, is not unreasonable; and its probability is reinforced by the stated fact that in both Chinese and Japanese dictionaries an ideograph combined of elements meaning respectively 'jewel' and 'moon' is defined as 'moon-pearl.'

I am inclined to regard this as a better explanation of the puzzling object so constantly associated with dragons in Chinese decorative art than is the 'thunder' hypothesis. At the same time it is to be noted that the spiral character of the 'pearl,' and of the 'tag' that springs from its centre, is the widely recognized symbol for thunder; while the antler-like appendages indicate accompanying lightnings; therefore the identification of the 'pearl' with the moon need not preclude its co-association with thunderstorms, for the dragon is a rain-controller, and in a fair sense is the deity heard and seen in thunder and lightning, who is in particular the storm-god of sailormen.

In Japan, whose dragon-mythology has been strongly tinctured with Indian notions, as we have seen, the pearl appears mainly in connection with mythical tales of the ocean—a very natural connection. In the *Nihongi,* an ancient Japanese historical work, it is related that in the second year of the Emperor Chaui's reign (A.D. 193) the Empress Jingo-Kogo found in the sea "a jewel which grants all desires," apparently the same lost by the frightened Naga Maidens. She also obtained from the submarine palace of the dragon-king the ebb-jewel (*kan-ja*) and the flood-jewel (*man-ja*), by which she was able, on at least one important occasion, to control the tides; they are described in the *Nihongi* as about five *sun* long, the former white and the latter blue—the colour of the east, whence rain comes; and the moon is controller of the oceanic tides!

Japanese legends relating to this matter, as briefly given by Joly, in his elaborate work on the legendary art of Japan, are connected with the mythical character Riujin, the ruler of the waters of the globe, whose home is beneath the sea, or in deep lakes, and who is represented as a very old man bearing a coiled dragon on his head or back. Riujin carries the divine jewel *tama*, esteemed as a symbol of purity and usually shown in Japan on the forehead of the dragon; also the jewels of the flowing and the retreating tides, which he gave to Jingo-Kogo, Hikohodermi, and others.

In representations of Hendaka Sonja, one of the worshipful sixteen arhats, special disciples of Buddha, "he is generally shown," Joly tells us, "with a bowl from which issues a dragon or a rain-cloud. He holds the bowl aloft with his left hand and with his right carries the sacred gem. Sometimes he is shown seated on a rock, the dragon occasionally aside, and crouching to reach the *tama*."

Another legend relates that Riujin once captured from the Chinese queen, the daughter of Kamatari, a most precious jewel, which later was recovered from Riujin by a fisher-girl, wife of Kamatari, who went to the dragon's submarine palace and got possession of the gem. She immediately stabbed her breast and hid the jewel in the wound, then floated to the surface and was found by Kamatari, the jewel guiding him to her by the dazzling light it shed from the concealing wound that became fatal to the heroine. Such stories are logical if the 'jewel' (tama, pearl) is identified with the moon.

Now it may well be asked: how is it that, granting the fondness of dragons for gems and the identity of the several gems and jewels mentioned in myths and ceremonies, they all trace back in significance to the pearl? Well, the pearl is an excellent image in miniature of the full moon; it, like the moon, represents water, and is a part of the history of the sea

116

LACQUER PEDESTAL AND BRONZE SWORDGUARD.
Japanese, nineteenth century. Courtesy of the
Metropolitan Museum.

and sea-wanderings. Hence pearls were regarded as in the special possession of the sea-gods and water-spirits; and these beings were often pictured in forms far more fishy, or croco-dilian, or shark-like, than were the terrestrial, serpentine drag-ons. But Japanese mythology includes also an earthquake-fish (*Namazu*) like an eel, with a long, attenuated head and long feelers on both sides of the mouth, which stirs about under-ground, thus causing earthquakes.

"The cultural drift from West to East, along the south coast of India," Dr. Smith reminds us, "was effected mainly by sailors who were searching for pearls. Sharks constituted the special dangers the divers had to incur in exploiting pearl-beds to obtain the precious 'giver of life.' But at the time these great enterprises were undertaken in the Indian Ocean the people dwelling in the neighbourhood of the chief pearl-beds regarded the sea as the great source of all life-giving, and the god who exercised these powers was incarnated in a fish (ancestor of Dagon). The sharks therefore had to be brought into this scheme, and they were rationalized as the guardians of the storehouse of life-giving pearls at the bottom of the sea. . . . Out of these crude materials the imaginations of the early pearl-fishers created the picture of wonderful sub-marine palaces of Naga kings in which vast wealth, not merely of pearls but also of gold, precious stones, and beautiful maid-ens, were placed under the protection of shark-dragons."

Chapter Eleven

THE DRAGON INVADES THE WEST

AN ENTIRELY new field of research lies before us in the West —in Europe. There the word 'dragon' is as familiar as in China, but its form and connotations are decidedly different. Certainly civilization began much farther back in time in Egypt and Iraq, India and China, and the object of our curiosity took form in the Orient long before its image appeared in the West, but was it invented anew in Europe, or was it brought in? If imported, whence? and how?

The earliest traces of European civilization belong to Greece, and the oldest indication of the Mediterranean man's thoughts about great mysteries is given in the hero-tales that have come down to us from that history-laden peninsula and its islands. These ancient and cloudy myths imply that "in those days" the earth was possessed by a race of Titans, giants huge and fierce, whose bodies below the waist were supported by a pair of thick serpent-tails instead of legs, reminding us of those pictures of mythical forerunners of Chinese tribes engraved on the tombs of the ancestors of the Wu family in Shantung; and the Titans' wives were the Lamiæ—abominable hags. The chief God of that time was Ophion, the Great Snake; and it is difficult in studying these primitive fables to distinguish between the 'giants' of some stories and the 'dragons' of others: they seem to be the same. It was the task of newcomers, heroes bringing foreign gods, to conquer the giants and to enthrone on Olympus wholly human figures of power in place of the monstrous Ophion and his reptilian hosts. Saturn and Neptune (himself half man, half fish), and after them Zeus the sky-god, struggled for mastery of the world, and famous deeds against giants and dragons were performed by the Olympian heroes before Greece was rid of them.

Now, if all this ophidian prehistory was an original conception of the primitive inhabitants of eastern Greece, where the incidents seem to have been laid, and was remembered in tradition and folklore down to the time of Homer, the fact is remarkable, because no real serpent exists on the coasts or islands of the Ægean Sea, or on the mainland of Greece, that has large size or would inspire either fear or respect worth mention. The only venomous snake thereabout is the small viper common all over the warmer half of Europe. Are we not, rather, considering dim, distorted recollections of serpent-worshipping aborigines, for whom, if needed, there had been no lack of teachers during unnumbered previous centuries? Long before the days of Homer and Hesiod, or of the annalists and singers of Palestine, Egyptian and Syrian navigators were sailing about the Ægean Sea and between India and Egypt. They brought ideas from the East as well as goods. Nomadic 'Aryan' tribes were migrating with their flocks back and forth, as the seasons and pasturage changed, all over the plains between Thessaly and the highlands of Scythia and far Bactria. When they met other migrants and related tales of scenes and adventures in far countries, they told of strange gods and demons—half-human serpents often gigantic and terrible. With the dramatic sense strong in all primitive story-tellers, they gar-

119

nished their reports with marvels undreamed-of by their listeners, and to be effectively enlarged when retold by the shepherds and fishermen of Macedonia, or among the Attic hills, or in the 'isles of Greece.' From such narratives, probably "all made out of the carver's brain," were developed the queer and often horrid conceptions that took shape in the mythology of almost prehistoric Greece, and afterward these were seized upon as 'material' in symbolic art and epic poetry.

The oldest definite traces of the dragon in Europe are in the Greek legend, preserved by Homer and Hesiod, of Cadmus and his band of adventurers—probably some long-remembered incursion of raiders from the eastward; and, judging by his fancied presentment on a vase exhumed at Palermo, he was a wholly human warrior, and not at all like Cecrops, the mythical founder of Athens, a being whose body terminated in the shape of a fat and scaly serpent. As Seiffert condenses the legend, Cadmus, having been led by a magic cow to a spot in Bœotia where he was thus impelled to plant his intended colony, proposed to dedicate the site at once by the sacrifice of a (or perhaps *the*) cow—a distinctly Aryan proceeding. Therefore he sent his companions for the necessary pure water to a near-by spring, where all were immediately slain by a huge serpent, the dragon-guard of the fountain. This incident is quite in accord with Asiatic ideas of the time regarding dragon-serpents' functions. As soon as Cadmus learned of the slaughter of his comrades he rushed to the spring and killed the dragon; then, at the command of an invisible voice (some say of Athene), he drew out its teeth and 'sowed' them over the adjacent ground. A host of armed men immediately sprang up, each from one of the broadcast teeth, who instantly began to fight and slay one another until only five remained alive.

These survivors then quieted their fury and helped Cadmus build a stronghold, which finally developed into the city of Thebes. The five naturally became the ancestors of the Theban aristocracy, and one of them, Echion, called 'the serpent's son,' married Cadmus's daughter Agave. After many troubles King Cadmus retired to Illyria, where at last he and his wife Harmonia were changed into snakes, died, and were carried by the gods to the place of the blest. This *dénouement* is very inconsistent, but it shows how the "trail of the serpent" lies over every incident and fancy in that fantastic infancy-story of Hellas.

One cannot gather from the writings of the early poets and chroniclers any distinct idea of the traditional or supposed appearance of the monsters with which the sun-gods were incessantly battling, except that whenever a chance glimpse is permitted one sees the serpent-likeness. Such was Python, half man, half snake, as some say, which haunted the caves on Mt. Parnassus, particularly that cleft in the rocks, originally called Pytho, where afterward was established the Delphic oracle. Apollo seized the place just after his birth, slaying Python with the first arrows from his infant bow; and in later times a festival was held there every year at which the whole story was represented in pageantry—the prototype of similar historic festivals celebrated during the Middle Ages in Europe and not yet quite obsolete.

Python was one of the offspring of Typhœus and Echidna, themselves apparently son and daughter of Tartarus (underworld) and Gæa (earth). Echidna was part woman and part snake, and her brother-husband is identified with the Typhon of Egyptian mythology, otherwise Apop, one of the forms of wicked Set and a sort of duplicate of the Persian Azhi-Zohak, since he also is a gigantic demon, and has snakes sprouting from his shoulders. This diabolical pair further afflicted the world by engendering, in addition to Python, the three-headed dogs Orthos and Cerberus, the lion of Namæa, the Lernean hydra, the guardians of the orchards of Hesperus and of the Golden Fleece in Colchis, and perhaps other monsters of fable.

The most notable, perhaps, of this horrid brood was Hydra, a water-fiend that infested the region about Lake Lerna, near Argos, where it devastated the country of cattle and sheep, and whose breath even was a deadly poison. All accounts agree that it was an enormous water-snake with many heads—a hundred according to Diodorus, fifty says Eumenides, but the accepted opinion is that its heads numbered nine, one of which was believed to be immortal. To destroy this dreadful creature was thought worthy to be one of a dozen or so 'labours' assigned to Heracles (as tests of manhood?) by the Delphic oracle; and it was the only feat of the lot that he could not accomplish without help, because whenever one of the hydra's heads had been amputated two new ones would sprout in its place unless the wound were scarified by fire. Having scared the hydra out of its lair among the reeds by shooting at it fiery arrows, Heracles hewed at its heads, and as fast as he cut them off his nephew and charioteer, Iolaus, seared the bleeding stumps with a burning-iron. The hydra having at last been totally decapitated, the heroes piled a huge stone on its 'immortal' head and so prevented resuscitation of the evil.

A later and lesser sort of hydra was the chimæra, of which we may read in the *Iliad,* and which appears on the monuments "with the body of a serpent terminating in a head, and having two other heads as well, one a lion's in the usual place, the other a goat's rising out of the centre of the body. No one could overcome the chimæra, and it caused the death of many men by the fire it exhaled, until at last Bellerophon slew it."

The hydra seems to me a mere extravagance of the serpent-cult, not at all different from the Hindoos' many-headed nagas, and probably akin to them in history. Again, is the chimæra anything but a caricature of Marduk's sea-goat? The inference seems irresistible that the religious notions of the aborigines of Macedonia and prehistoric Greece were derived from India, by way of the wandering 'Aryans' of Thrace and the northern plains, tinctured with somewhat of the mythology of Egypt and Chaldea.

It has been said that the hydra was copied from the *poulpe,* or octopus, which infests the rocky shores and shallows of the eastern Mediterranean, but this seems to me improbable, however much the octopus may be recognized in certain other aspects of the myths and conventional designs characteristic of the Mediterranean region. More logically this repulsive cephalopod might well be regarded as the parent of the marine monster Scylla, finally exterminated by Heracles. She is described by Homer as dwelling on a tall rock in the sea where the lower half of her body is concealed in a cavern, whence she reaches out six long necks, each bearing a horrid head with three rows of teeth closely set (like the suckers of the cuttle), by which she catches fishes and other marine creatures, and snatches men off passing ships. (In later times she personified one of the two great perils in the navigation of the Strait of Messina.)

It is needless to catalogue all the misshapen and fearful monsters recorded in the legends found in the writings of Homer and Hesiod, and revived by Ovid and the later poets and artists of Greece and Rome. Heracles, Perseus, Theseus and other heroes arose to kill them off when a developing civilization and humourous skepticism required their extinction. Meleager freed the peasantry from the ravages of a gigantic boar. Heracles slew the huge Nemæan lion, dispersed the man-eating Stymphalian birds, and overcame in amazing battles several giants, such as Cacus and the river-god Achelous, who nearly escaped by transforming himself into a snake; and captured the Island of the Hesperides from the hundred-headed serpent Ladon, protector of the golden apples that Gæa had cultivated as a wedding gift for Hera when Zeus should marry her in this garden of the gods. Ladon, expelled from earth, was set up in the sky by Juno as the constellation known to us as The Serpent. Extremely ancient is the tale of the Argonauts, which has so many features in common with that of Cadmus, and records Jason's final achievement of their purpose by vanquishing the dragon that held the post of custodian of the coveted golden fleece, and who was the last of the progeny of Echidna and Typhon. Finally Perseus, by conquering a prodigious sea-serpent, rescued the forlorn but interesting maid Andromeda, and thereby became the remotest ancestor of all the redoubtable 'Saint-Georges' whose adventures are in store for us. Trail of the serpent again!

Perseus became the son of Zeus and Danæ, after Zeus had visited her in the guise of a shower of gold poured into her lap. He had many adventures, including the killing of Medusa, the chief of the snaky-locked Gorgons, but the heroic incident that interests us most is his saving of Andromeda. This unhappy maid was a daughter of Cepheus and Cassiopeia. Cassiopeia had boasted herself fairer than the Nereids, whereupon Poseidon, the sea-god, to punish this profanity, sent a flood to overwhelm the land and a sea-monster to consume the people.

The oracle of Ammon promised riddance of the plague should Andromeda be thrown to the monster (represented in a sculpture of the classic period, preserved in the Capitoline Museum in Rome, as a big, pike-like fish); Cepheus therefore felt compelled to chain his daughter to a rock on the shore, convenient to the marine 'dragon' when the tide rose. In this distressful situation Perseus appears, full of gallantry, destroys the approaching monster, and having thus rescued her and freed the threatened country, obtained the girl as his wife. The legend of Heracles and Hesione is virtually the same.

These 'snake-stories' and other figments of the imagination of a rude and adventurous people would have been forgotten long, long ago, had not their dramatic possibilities been seen and utilized by the early bards to enrich the more or less rhythmical stories they chanted in village huts and by the shepherds' camp-fire, not to mention their use by the early vase-painters. Considering these matters in his valuable treatise on modern Greek folklore, Mr. John C. Lawson [23] has distinguished several kinds or classes of genii visible in the fables and folk-tales of the Hellenic people past and present.

The third class of genii [he remarks], is terrestrial, inhabiting mountains, rocks, caves, and other grim and desolate places. These genii are the most frequent of all, and are known as dragons. Not, of course, that all dragons are terrestrial; the dragon form has already been mentioned as among the forms proper to the genii of springs and wells. . . . The term drakos *or* drakontas *indicates to the Greek peasant a monster of no more determinate shape than does 'dragon' among ourselves. The Greek word, however, . . . is often employed in a strict and narrow sense to denote a 'serpent' as distin-*

guished from a small snake (phodi). *On the other hand a Greek 'dragon' in the widest sense of the word is sometimes distinctly anthropomorphic in popular stories, and is made to boil kettles and drink coffee without any sense of impropriety. It is in fact only from the context of the story that it is possible to tell in what shape the dragon is imagined; in general it is neither flesh, fowl nor good red devil; heads and tails, wings and legs, teeth and talons, are assigned to it in any number and variety; it sleeps with its eyes open, and sees with them shut; it makes war on men and love to women; it roars or it sings; . . . . it is the dragon above all other supernatural beings, who provides the wandering hero of the fairy-tales with befitting adventures and tests of prowess.*

Now, a striking feature of this whole race of prehistoric Greek 'dragons' is that they have no lizard-like, four-footed body, no kindliness of disposition, and nothing to do with rainfall or productivity of the soil. The exception to complete dissimilarity with the Chinese variety is that some of them have the office of guardians of women and treasure. On the other hand these fierce and horrid 'Pelasgian' creatures of a lively imagination portray, far more evidently than do the Oriental 'dragons,' the fears and emotions of a people half-savage, it is true, yet possessed of an alertness of mind very different from the rather bovine and 'single-track' mentality of the Hindoos and Chinese. The varied personages and adventures of the Greek hero-stories appeal in one way or another to us as they did to the men of antiquity (and as the Oriental ones do not); and this must account both for their seizure and preservation for us by the poets and artists between us and them in time, and for their present power to move us as symbols of things

126

we feel and understand, though long disregarded as facts. A similar quality of dramatic reality belongs to much of the Persian mythology, and this strengthens the theory that Greece derived these notions from the prehistoric men of central Asia overland, rather than from Asia Minor by way of the Ægean islands, or to any great extent from Egypt by way of Crete— the latter in later times the channel of an invigorating influence.

Yet one cannot be sure that the Egyptian demonology did not tincture the superstition of the earliest Greeks, for prehistoric sculptures exhumed in Crete show water-demons of queerly changed crocodilian aspect with strange mammalian heads, and distinctly four-legged, which might have served as prototypes of the forms later developed in western Europe.

The Hittites and Phœnicians do not appear to have had in their history or religion any proper dragons, for their fiendish Moloch was certainly not of that (Chaldean) race; hence nothing of the sort has been revealed in Carthage or in the remains of other Phœnician settlements on the shores of the Mediterranean.

All the foregoing matter is mythical or legendary. We get upon fairly firm ground of fact about fifteen centuries before the Christian era, when invaders from the north penetrated the Epirus, expelled or subdued the barbarous 'Pelasgians,' and established themselves as settlers and rulers. These conquerors, known henceforth as Achæans, were Nordic tribes of somewhat superior physique and culture, speaking an Aryan dialect out of which the Greek language developed. With their advent the history of the country begins, and the aboriginal stories of dragons, giants, and incredible heroes fade rapidly into folklore and become merely literary and artistic materials. Camps and caves are replaced by substantial buildings, and these become improved into the splendid edifices of the Golden Age of Greek art. It is noteworthy at this point to remark that from the very beginning in megalithic or 'Mycænian' structures the ornamentation of neither temples, official buildings, nor private houses had any suggestion of the ancient serpent-cult, unlike what has happened in China and Japan, where images of dragons and snakes meet the eye in every city and village and keep alive their sacred and symbolic significance. Even statuary and decorative designing among the Greeks almost completely ignored this temptingly useful material, evidently rejected on grounds of good taste because of the unpleasant suggestions involved in everything reptilian. The horrifying figures of the Laocoön form a notable exception, but there the terrible serpent is an image of a real snake, not one derived from a myth.

When, in its decadence, Greece sank into the Roman empire, its legends were absorbed along with its lands, but the Romans were a very hard-headed people (apart from their day-by-day watching for omens), and having thrown away long before such antique lumber as dragon-tales—if ever they had any— they were not inclined to adopt any new ones from a neigh- bour's garret, save as here and there a small and picturesque bit might be worth saving as a 'museum-piece' of folklore or poetry. They still held to some relics of serpent worship, such as the attribution of snakes to Apollo and to Æsculapius, and their connection with the cult of the Lares, or household gods, under the impression that these house-haunting mouse-hunters were guardian spirits, whence images of them were hung up in shrines—for luck! But Lares were not dragons. The near- est approach to our subject appears to be the fable of the basilisk or cockatrice, and that I judge to be of Egyptian origin, and made up of travellers' tales about spitting vipers; at best this undesirable creature was nothing but a venomous serpent endowed with supernatural qualities.

That they knew in Rome what a proper dragon looked like is plain from the engravings that remain of the standard of one of the legions in the Roman army. The Rev. J. B. Deane,[24] whose old book bears the appearance of patient care, assures his readers that at the time when Rome was growing up the warriors of the Persians, Scythians, Parthians, Assyrians, and even the Saxons, "had dragon standards"; he explains also, quoting Latin writers of the age of the Caesars, that in the army of Marcus Aurelius, and afterward, flag-like images woven into the shape of a traditional dragon, were carried by each of the ten companies (cohorts) in a regiment (legion), whose regimental standard represented an eagle. Later, the dragon emblem was taken from the regular army and, in its Parthian form, was adopted as the general standard for the Auxiliary Corps. Thus in time it became the ensign of the emperors of the West whose troops were wholly Auxiliaries; and in the painting in the Vatican depicting Constantine the Great announcing to his soldiers his conversion to Christianity, a buoyant image of a winged, four-footed, proper dragon is prominently displayed, floating from a lofty pike-head.

With the 'decline and fall' of Rome, then, knowledge of the dragon might have disappeared from the western world forever had it not been revived at the last gasp, as it were, in the interest of Christianity and in the person of His Eminence the Devil.

Chapter Twelve

THE 'OLD SERPENT' AND HIS PROGENY

IT IS difficult to determine whether the Hebrews, as we know them in the Bible, believed in the actual existence of what we call a 'dragon,' at least as resident in Palestine. "Hebrew theology," Geiger concludes, "had no demonology or Satan until after the residence at Babylon. . . . The account of the Garden of Eden dates from a time subsequent to the captivity"; and this eminent expositor assumes that Satan came from the Zoroastrian conception of Arhiman, "the evil serpent bearing death."

The features of the original Sumerian, or pre-Sumerian, myth of the struggle of Marduk with Tiamat had become considerably modified by that time even in Babylonia. Dr. Ward mentions a cylinder on which Bel-Marduk is depicted as chasing and killing the Evil One—an unmistakable serpent. "This," Dr. Ward thought, "is convincing proof that in the region where it was made the spirit of evil was conceived as a serpent, as it is in *Genesis*, and also in *Job* 26:13 and *Isaiah* 27:1." Job calls it a 'crooked serpent,' and Isaiah declares that in due time the Lord of Israel "shall punish the leviathan, that crooked serpent; and he shall slay the leviathan that is in the sea."

Most of the allusions in the Old Testament appear to be allegorical or poetic, 'dragon' merely serving with the owl, raven, and other creatures of the Syrian wilderness as an expression for desert desolation. The prophets and bards, ad-

130

dressing a people fond of figurative speech, were no doubt confident their allusions and metaphors would be understood, even when a devouring, malignant, and unearthly agent of evil was meant, as in the frightful visions limned by the excited author of the *Book of Revelations*. Take, for example, John's vision in Patmos of dragon-horses (*Rev.* 9:17) whose heads "were as the heads of lions; and out of their mouths issued fire and smoke and brimstone . . . for their power is in their mouth and in their tails, for their tails are like unto serpents, and had heads, and with them they do hurt."

Then there is that powerful modern picture in enduring phrases: "There was war in heaven: Michael and his angels fought against the dragon; and the dragon fought and his angels, and prevailed not; neither was their place found any more in heaven. And the great dragon was cast out, that old serpent called the Devil and Satan, which deceiveth the whole world; he was cast out and his angels were cast with him." Milton in next describing Satan's return to Pandemonium, changed to a dragon, finely distinguishes this hellish monster from the snaky tribe out of which it has grown, in these verses from *Paradise Lost* (10: 519):

> *For now were all transformed*
> *Alike, to serpents all, as accessories*
> *To his bold riot. Dreadful was the din*
> *Of hissing through the hall, thick-swarming now*
> *With complicated monsters head and tail,*
> *Scorpion, and asp, and amphisbæna dire,*
> *Cerastes horned, hydrus and ellops drear,*
> *And dipsas (not so thick swarmed once the soil*
> *Bedropt with blood of gorgon, or the isle*

Ophiusa); but still greatest he the midst,
Now dragon grown, larger than whom the sun
Engendered in the Pythian vale on slime,
Huge Python; and his power no less he seemed
Above the rest still to retain.

The figures of metaphor chosen by St. John show that he knew the traditional characteristics (largely derived from India) of these reptilian ogres, and counted on the public's familiarity with them. No doubt he had often heard or read dozens of legends about them—such tales, for example, as the following one recounted in the long story about Job by Thal'labi, who died in 1035 A.D. It is a part of the *Book of the Stories of the Poets,* from which it was quoted into the American Journal of Semitic Languages (vol. 13, p. 145). God is haranguing the fretful Job:

"Where wast thou in the day when I formed the dragon? His food is in the sea and his dwelling in the air; his eyes flash fire; his ears are like the bow of the clouds, there pours forth from them flame as though he were a whirling wind-column of dust; his belly burns and his breath flames forth in hot coals like unto rocks; it is as though the clash of his teeth were sounds of thunder and the glance of his eye were the flashing of lightning; armies pass him while he is lying; nothing terrifies him; in him there is no joint . . . he destroys all that by which he passes."

The rendering by the English word 'dragon' in the authorized version of the Bible of both the two similar words *tan* and *thanin* is explained by Canon Tristram in his authentic *Natural History of the Bible.* "*Tan,*" he announces, "is al-

THE DRAGON OF THE CLOISTERS.

ST. MICHAEL.

French stone sculptures of the fourteenth and fifteenth centuries.

Courtesy of the Metropolitan Museum.

ways used in the plural for some creature inhabiting desert places, frequently coupled with the ostrich and wild beasts." The Prophets and Psalmist abound in such references, and hear their cries from the most desolate haunts they are able to picture to their minds. "I will make a wailing like the dragons, and mourning as the ostriches," exclaims Micah, remembering nocturnal voices that had echoed in the desert from ghostly ruins and perilous wastes—voices of real animals such as jackals, whose mournful howlings disturb the nervous and superstitious, or owls, always troublesome to timorous souls.

The writer of the article 'Dragon' in the *Jewish Cyclopedia* informs us that in the Septuagint version the word signifies a dangerous monster whose bite is poisonous. This accords with the Hindoo definition of a naga, which designates a venomous snake alone, a cobra. Such monsters must be imagined, says this Hebrew commentator, as of composite but snake-like form, and always as at home in water, even in the waves of the sea (*Psalms* 48: 7), where they were created by God with the fishes. "In the beginning of things YHWH overpowered them in creating the world. It is clear that this story, which is found only in fragments in the O. T., was originally a myth representing God's victory over the seas."

The hot and arid country of the Holy Land was particularly favourable to serpent life. Several venomous species were present then as now, lurking not only in thickets and hedges (*Eccl.* 10: 8), and among rocks, but even in and about the rude, stone-built, dark houses of Judean villages, where they crept in search of mice, insects, etc. Amos alludes warningly to the danger in leaning against a house-wall lest an unseen serpent bite the lounger. Men saw the snake crawling in the dust, and held as a fact that it had been cursed in Eden

(*Genesis* 3:14) to travel forever on its belly as a mark of degradation; only wondering why, instead, the good Lord had not removed altogether so dangerous a pest from his chosen people. Add to this power for harm its traditional history as something impious, and nothing seems more natural to a zoologist or an anthropologist than that this sly reptile should typify the unseen and dire influences that we name Eblis, Satan, the Devil, the Old Serpent, and so forth, and should become the prototype of the Dragon of Biblical and hence of modern legendary love, almost independently of Far Eastern notions.

Faiths, traditions, and figures of speech relating to these matters were an important element in the Christianity brought to Rome by early Jewish propagandists of the new religion, a striking novelty in which was the doctrine of punishment after death for wickedness wrought in life. No longer were men taught that when life ceased their spiritual selves were transported to another world more or less like this one; on the contrary they were sternly warned that if they died in their sins they went to a place of eternal suffering in charge of a supreme torturer, who daily went roaming about on earth in ingenious and subtle disguises, tempting men to put themselves everlastingly in his power. He was called chiefly 'Satan' and 'Devil.' Both these names were terms taken from Oriental languages, and naturally soon came to be concretely represented by the figure of the Eastern dragon, with whom the populace, grown acquainted with Oriental things by the empire's conquests in Asia Minor and Persia, was vaguely familiar.

To fully identify this dragon of tradition with the Devil of the Bible, and so increase the terror of his power, was easy to the zealous, if not over-wise, ministers of Chistianity, and evidence of their success is found in the many representations in mediæval religious art to be seen in ancient books and manuscripts, numerous examples of which have been copied into Carus's *History of the Devil*[25] and other similar treatises.

"Set," remarks Dr. G. E. Smith, "the enemy of Osiris, who is the real prototype of the evil dragon, was the antithesis of the god of justice; he was the father of falsehood and the symbol of chaos. He was the prototype of Satan, as Osiris was the first definite representative of the Deity of which any record has been preserved. . . .

"The history of the evil dragon is not merely the evolution of the Devil, but it also affords the explanation of his traditional peculiarities, his bird-like features, his horns, his red color, his wings and cloven hoofs, and his tail. They are all of them the dragon's distinctive features; and from time to time in the history of past ages we catch glimpses of the reality of these identifications. In one of the earliest woodcuts found in a printed book Satan is represented as a monk with the bird's feet of the dragon. A most interesting intermediate phase is seen in a Chinese watercolor in the John Rylands Library (at Manchester, England), in which the thunder-dragon is represented in a form almost exactly reproducing that of the Devil of European tradition."

Here we have the genesis of the figure of Mephistopheles! In the oldest version of the Faust legend (sixteenth century) Mephistopheles, the servant-devil, sends Faust through the air whithersoever he wishes to go, according to their compact, on a carriage drawn by dragons, not by wafting him on a magic cloak, as in the more modern rendering.

Dr. Smith continues: "Early in the Christian era, when ancient beliefs in Egypt became disguised under a thin veneer of Christianity, the story of the conflict between Horus and Set was converted into a conflict between Christ and Satan. M. Clermont Ganneau has described an interesting bas-relief in the Louvre in which a hawk-headed St. George, clad in Roman military uniform and mounted on a horse, is slaying a dragon which is represented by Set's crocodile. But the Biblical references to Satan leave no doubt as to his identity with the dragon, who is specifically mentioned in the *Book of Revelations* as 'the Old Serpent, which is the devil and Satan.' "

As Greco-Roman-born civilization gradually displaced savagery and barbarism throughout Europe, the idea expressed by the modern term 'dragon' spread with it in two streams and with two meanings, but lost much of its religious significance.

The eldest of these streams, derived from a prehistoric Asiatic source, was carried westward in that steady movement of eastern tribes which began to be felt along the Danube about ten thousand years ago, and slowly pressed forward to the Atlantic coast. This Neolithic current of rude, yet superior men and women, brought with it, along with certain arts and customs of a settled life, faith in and awe of a more or less demonic serpent connected with the guardianship of springs, rivers, and waters generally, but which was not much concerned with rainfall, for these early invaders of central Europe had little reason for anxiety as to sufficient rain for their simple gardening or pasturage. Later came invasions of Europe by ruder migrants from Scythia. Sarmatia, and other oriental tribes and regions.

The other stream of ideas proceeded at a later time from Christianized Italy by means of Roman soldiers (who carried an image of the dragon on their lances), or by wandering missionaries of the Church inculcating among the peoples north of the Alps religious creeds and allegories in which the dragon became a symbol and representative of the Biblical devil, and hence of all enemies of 'the true faith,' especially heresy and heathenism. Archæologists find that all over eastern Europe, even to within historic times, reverence was paid to serpents, partly in a worshipful way, partly with superstitious dread—a universal characteristic of primitive religions which reached its highest development in the tropics, where great and formidable snakes inspired just respect. This prevailed, as we know, among the plainsmen of southeastern Asia and on the Russian steppes, but affected very little the tribes of the forested country west of Russia.

Hence in Europe the presentation of the dragon as the Spirit of Evil and Anti-Christ, in a garb borrowed from Hebrew imagery and the visions of the *Book of Revelations,* easily superseded aboriginal notions yet, especially in the north and in the mountainous eastern borderland, was never wholly freed from them.

In his *Zoological Mythology* Angelo de Gubernatis presents many facts of modern Balkan and Russian folklore showing coördination with Hindoo theology. A story from Serbian folktales quoted in Frazer's *Folklore in the Old Testament* tells how a human giant of great ferocity, the owner of a mill, was wheedled by a woman until he revealed where his strength lay —as follows:

Far in another kingdom, under the king's city, is a lake; in the lake is a dragon; in the dragon is a boar; in the boar is a pigeon, and in the pigeon is my strength." A prince, whose *two brothers the ogre had killed, learned this fact from the woman and made his way to the lake, where, after a terrible*

*tussle, he slew the water-dragon and extracted the pigeon.
Having questioned the pigeon, and ascertained from it how
to restore his two murdered brothers, to life, the prince wrung
the bird's neck, and no doubt the wicked dragon [of the mill]
perished miserably at the same moment.*

Craigie,[26] writing of Scandinavian folklore, says that stories
of dragons that fly through the air by night and vomit fire are
fairly common in Norway and Denmark, and are not unknown
in England. "In various places all over the country there are
still shown holes in the earth out of which they are seen to
come flying like blazing fire when wars or other troubles
are to be expected. When they return to their dwellings, where
they brood over immense treasures (which they, as some say,
have gathered by night in the depths of the sea), there can be
heard the clang of the great iron doors that close behind them."

Not only do these fiery, long-tailed dragons fly about, but
terrestrial ones still brood over piles of gold coins in mounds
and beneath churches. When they appear, as they sometimes
do, various recipes exist for forcing them to reveal or even to
shower down their gold, but the conditions accompanying these
instructions are usually impossible to fulfil. The 'lindorms'
and 'king-vipers' mentioned by Craigie are said to be serpents,
usually of great size, that do various sorts of mischief, one
kind having ghoulish habits; and these malicious beings are almost always connected in some way with imaginary bulls—an
association constantly observed in serpent-myths, and undoubtedly indicating a phallic significance.

Frazer quotes (*Balder*, Vol. I) a mediæval writer who
recorded that in some parts of Europe on Midsummer Night
it was the custom to burn bones and filth to make a foul

ST. GEORGE SLAYING A FLYING DRAGON.

Dutch, fifteenth century.

smudge, because this smoke drove away "certain noxious dragons which at this time, excited by the summer heat, copulated in the air and poisoned the wells and rivers by dropping their seed into them."

Grimm adds such items of Teutonic lore as follow. The dragon lives 90 years in the ground, 90 in the lime-tree, and 90 more in the desert, sunning his gold in fine weather. Heimo finds a dragon in the Alps of Carneola, kills it and cuts out its tongue, and with the tongue in hand finds a rich hoard. The swords of Sigurd and of Alexander (the Great?) were tempered in dragon's blood, which when eaten confers a knowledge of the language of birds, which are messengers of the gods.* Dragons are hated; but it is a German saying that a venom-spitting dragon can blow its poison through seven church-walls but not through knitted stockings.

Such are dozens of living northern stories and fancies, traceable back into an almost forgotten antiquity.

Very old and primitive is the Teutonic tale of the dragons of the Underworld which come flying toward the shades of the dead, trying to obstruct their advance when on their way to the realm of a blissful eternity. There were also dragons on earth as well as beneath it; and one of these has survived to serve on the operatic stage wherever Wagner's *Nibelungen* series is produced. This is the story as recited in the *Saga* of Volsung—a German epic of unknown authorship produced about the end of the 12th century: The great god Wotan (or Odin) is possessed of a vast treasure which is committed by the gods into the keeping of two giants. One of them, Fafnir, kills his brother in order to get possession of all the wealth, and then

* See my book *Birds in Legend, Fable and Folklore* (New York, 1923).

transforms himself into a dragon to guard it. Wotan wants to recover his treasure. A knight, Siegfried (Norse, Sigurd) forges a magical sword out of the pieces of his father's sword 'Nothing.' Wotan and his brother Alberich come to where the dragon Fafnir is watching over the stolen money and jewels, including a magic ring belonging to Alberich to which a curse is attached. Siegfried approaches the horrid lair, whereupon Fafnir comes out, and in the fight that ensues Siegfried slays the beast by aid of his magic sword. The king tells the hero about the ring, and Siegfried goes and gets it, but its possession insures him constant trouble and unhappiness. Everyone regards this 'dragon' as a demon in serpent form, and he is always so represented on the operatic stage, and in the illustrations accompanying the tale in the many books in which it has been recounted in prose and verse, for it is the favourite hero-myth of the Germans.

In the Norse saga of King Olaf the hero ploughs the northern seas in his viking boat and surprises and seizes the great freebooter Raud, who has been ravaging the shores of Norway in his 'dragon-boat.' That craft is destroyed, and Olaf then instructs the shipwrights to construct for his majesty a 'serpent-boat' twice as big. These were Norse sea-boats having tall figureheads of serpent-dragon form, in regard to which much that is entertaining is written in old books.

Chapter Thirteen

SUPERNATURAL BEASTS abound in the traditions and early records of the British Isles, and stand as ominous shades in the background of modern rural folklore, especially where the population is predominantly of Celtic descent. Celtic invaders from the continent possessed themselves of Ireland, Cornwall, Wales and western Scotland, even before the beginning of the Christian era, expelling or absorbing the previous native occupants, also many savage notions. They brought with them, and all sections share the substructure of, a body of faiths and fancies, poetic and superstitious, engaging demonic creatures, supermen and personifications of nature, that form a more or less unified mythology known to antiquarians as the great Celtic dragon-myth. Its stories, in which prehistoric fiction and legendary or real incidents and personages are inextricably mingled, abound in giants, semi-human ogres, serpents and dragons of land, water and air, sea-monsters, mermaids and fairies. J. F. Cambell [27] has devoted a whole book to this matter, and an awesome belief in much of its mystery still lingers among the peasantry about the Irish lakes, in the glens of wilder Wales, and among the lochs and sea-isles of Scotland. Dreadful 'warrums,' half fish, half dragon, still inhabit some Irish lakes, while on others the boatmen will speak with bated breath of monstrous beasts that formerly lurked in their depths; and

141

the 'water-horses' of certain Scottish lochs are near cousins to them.

Dragon or demon, raven or serpent, eagle or sleeping warriors, Mr. Wirt Sikes declares in his British Goblins, *the guardian of the underground vaults in Wales where treasures lie is a personification of the baleful influences which reside in caverns, graves and subterraneous regions generally. It is something more than this when traced back to its source in the primeval mythology; the dragon which watched the golden apples of Hesperides, and the Payshthamore, or great worm, which in Ireland guards the riches of O'Rourke, is the same malarious creature which St. Samson drove out of Wales. According to the monkish legend this pestiferous beast was of vast size, and by its deadly breath had destroyed two cities. It lay hid in a cave near the river. Thither went St. Samson accompanied only by a boy, and tied a linen girdle about the creature's neck, and drew it out and threw it headlong from a certain high eminence into the sea. This dreadful dragon became mild and gentle when addressed by the saint. . . . The mysterious beast of the boy Taliesin's song in the marvelous legend of Gwion Bach, told in the* The Mabinogion, *is a dragon worthy to be classed with the gigantic conceptions of primeval imagination, which sought by these prodigious figures to explain all the phenomena of nature. "A noxious creature from the ramparts of Santanas," sings Taliesin, "with jaws as wide as mountains; in the hair of its two paws there is the load of 900 wagons, and in the nape of its neck three springs arise, through which the sea-roughs swim."*

Cuchulain, the supreme Irish hero, who had to undergo Herculean tests of fortitude, was once attacked by such a beast

*of magic, which flew on horrible wings from a lake. Cuchu-
lain sprang up to meet it, giving his wonderful hero-leap, thrust
his arm into the dragon's mouth and down its throat and tore
out its heart. With figures from such legends as these Spenser
embellished his* Faery Queene, *picturing an*

*". . . ugly monster plaine,
Half like a serpent horribly displaide
But th' other half did woman's shape retaine,
Most lothsom, filthie, foule, and full of vile disdaine."*

A very ancient fragment of the Celtic myth still remembered among Scottish Gaels is the tale of Froach and the Rowan
Tree, preserved in the *Book of Linsmore*, a Gaelic text of the
sixteenth century. There was a king in the land whose wife
was named Mève, and they had a marriageable daughter, the
princess. The rowan (our mountain ash) stood among the
ancient Celts as 'the tree of life' because wondrous medicinal
virtues were believed to reside in its red berries; and the lesson
of the tale exhibits the sin and dire consequences of disturbing
its growth. The king with Queen Mève and their daughter
lived near a lake in the midst of which was an island on which
stood a rowan-tree guarded by a dragon, as is told in Henderson's translation [29] in verse of the old 'grete':

*A rowan tree grew on Loch Meve—
Southwards is seen the shore—
Every fourth and every month
Ripe fruit the rowan bore:
Fruit more sweet than honeycomb,
Its clusters virtues strong,
Its berries red could one but taste
Hunger they stand off long.*

Its berries' juice and fruit when red
For you would life prolong:
From dread disease it gave relief
If what is told be our belief.

Yet though it proved a means of life
Peril lay closely nigh;
Coiled by its root a dragon lay,
Forbidding passing by.

In the neighbourhood dwelt a young nobleman named Froach, the suitor of the king's daughter, who tells him that her mother, the queen, is ill, and that her only cure is in the berries of the rowan growing on the island as gathered by Froach's hands. Froach protested a little at the extreme peril of the task given him, but bravely agreed to try, and stripping off his clothes plunged in. Swimming to the island he gathered and brought back a goodly quantity of the ripe berries, unnoticed by the dragon. But Mève declared that they were useless—to cure her she must have a branch of the tree bearing fruit.

Froach gave consent; no fear he knew
But swam the lake once more;
But hero never yet did pass
The fate for him in store.

The rowan by the top he seized,
From root he pulled the tree;
And the monster of the lake perceived
As Froach from the land made free.

The dragon then attacked the hero, who had no weapon, "and shore away his arm." The princess seeing his plight, ran

into the water and gave the man a sword, with which he ultimately killed the brute; but his wounds were fatal, and he
reached the shore only to deliver the tree and the dragon's
head to the women, and to die at their feet. In another version,
however, Froach is nursed in the palace to recovery, outwits a
rival, and obtains the princess despite Queen Mève's illwill.

Very similar and more famous is the romance of Tristan
and Iseult, which was written out by Gottfried Strasburger, a
German poet who lived early in the thirteenth century. In
Ireland, his poem tells us, was once a dreadful dragon wasting
the land. The king swore a solemn oath that he would give
his daughter, Princess Iseult, to whatever man should slay it.
Many knights tried the feat, but lost their lives: always with
the candidate rode the seneschal of the palace, but always at
sight of the beast he ran away to safety. At last the knight
Tristan offered himself, and rode toward the dragon's den, accompanied by the seneschal, who turned back the moment danger appeared, but Tristan rode on steadily. "Ere long he saw
the monster coming towards him breathing out smoke and flame
from its open jaws. The knight laid his spear in rest and rode
so swiftly, and smote so strongly that the spear . . . pierced
through the throat into the dragon's heart." The beast was not
yet quite killed, however, and fled with Tristan's spear sticking
in its vitals. The knight followed fast, overtook the brute,
and a long and terrific fight ensued, "so fierce that the shield
he held in his hand was burnt well-nigh to a coal" by the
flames from the dragon's nostrils. Struggling painfully back
to the king's city, the exhausted hero fell into a pond and would
have drowned had not Iseult and her mother come by and
dragged him out. Then the cowardly seneschal asserted he
had done the glorious deed, whereupon Tristan shows the

tongue of the dragon as evidence of his own claim to the reward. This is an example of the many mediæval stories of later birth (progeny of Perseus), in which some untoward circumstance prevents the hero establishing his claim before an impostor has run before him to the court, yet wins in the end by means of concealed evidence.

The terms dragon, drake, serpent, worm, were more or less interchangeable in northern Europe, where even now you may hear described to you a fabulous *wurm-bett,* or serpent's bed, as the place of gold with a dragon-guardian. So it was in Britain, where this creature was associated with the exploits of the Round Table; for we find the following among the Arthurian legends which are more particularly Welsh: Merlin, the magician, was asked by King Vortigern (fifth century), how to render stable a tower of his castle which thrice had tumbled down. Merlin explained that the trouble lay in the fact that the tower had been built over the den of two immense dragons, whose combats shook the foundations above them. "The king ordered his workmen to dig," as Bulfinch [30] tells it, "and when they had done so they discovered two enormous serpents, the one white as milk, the other red as fire. The multitude looked on with amazement till the serpents, slowly rising from their den, and expanding their enormous folds, began the combat, when every one fled in terror except Merlin, who stood by, clapping his hands and cheering on the conflict. The red dragon was slain, and the white one, gliding through a cleft in the rock, disappeared."

This incident is reputed to have taken place on an isolated rocky eminence in Carnarvonshire, where remains of extensive prehistoric stone-works are still to be seen, says Rhys; in truth it is, of course, purely mythical.

146

"Whence came the red dragon of Cadwaladar? Why was the Welsh dragon in fables of Merddin (Merlin), Wennius, and Geofrey described as red, while the Saxon 'fenris' was white?" asks Mr. Sikes. He expresses his belief that there is no answer outside the realm of fancy, but notes that in the Welsh language *draig* means 'lightning,' while the *Welsh-English Dictionary* asserts that it symbolizes the sun. These might account for the ruddiness, but the facts are needless, for blood-red is the natural choice of warriors, and these fiery Welshmen seem to have preëmpted it in Britain. The dragon itself was perhaps that of Froach, the great Celtic hero—at any rate it was the device on the banners of the old Welsh kings, legendary and real, and was carried by Cadwaladar (or Caedwalla), king of North Wales, in his battles with Northumberland in the seventh century A.D. Those old warrior-kings had the title *Pendragon,* as Tennyson knew when in *Guinevere* he referred to the royal headquarters in the field—

> *They saw*
> *The dragon of the great Pendragon*
> *That crowned the state pavilion of the king.*

And Shakespeare writes: "Peace, Kent. Come not between the Dragon and his wrath."

This is the red, or sometimes golden, dragon that has been so closely associated with British royalty. The Black Prince flourished it over the heads of his soldiers at Crecy, and so it came to be recognized for many years as the badge of the Principality. New honours for the historic symbol naturally followed the accession of the Welsh Tudors to the English throne, for Henry VII, on his entry into London after his victory on Bosworth Field, offered at the altar in St. Paul's

147

cathedral a standard with the fiery dragon of Wales "beaten upon white and green sarcenet." This king then granted formally to King George, then Prince of Wales, and to his successors, a second badge, namely: "A red dragon with elevated wings, passant thereon, for difference a silver label of three points." This grant was continued by Henry VIII, Edward VI, Mary, and Elizabeth—the last named preferring as the supporter of her arms a golden figure with a narrow red back.

But the device on the Welsh flag was not invariably red— or perhaps the variation to be mentioned designated the South Welsh as distinct from those of the North; at any rate we read* among the Arthurian legends that in the time of Arthur's father, Uther, there appeared a star at Winchester of wonderful-magnitude brightness, "darting forth a ray at the end of which was a flame in form of a dragon." Uther then ordered two golden dragons to be made, one of which he presented to Winchester, and the other he carried with him as a royal standard. Arthur himself, it is stated, wore a dragon on the crest of his helmet—a tradition Spenser knew:

> His haughty helmet, horrid all with gold,
> > Both glorious brightness and great terror bred,
> For all the crest a dragon did enfold,
> > With greedy paws.

In historic times, the Roman soldiers in England carried images or pictures of dragons as ensigns in their wars with the native Britons. If these were mainly white that fact might account for the whiteness of the emblems used by the 'Saxon' armies of the South (Sussex), with which, after the Roman troops had quit England, the west-central kingdom, Wessex, was incessantly in conflict. Wessex, supported by the southern

MEDIÆVAL CELTIC DRAGON (SIXTH CENTURY) WITH TWO HERALDIC WELSH DRAGONS.

149

Welsh, fought under a 'golden' banner, and the adoption of a white-dragon flag by the Sussex men may have been merely a matter of useful distinction between the opposing forces.

It was the Wessex men under Harold that finally expelled the Norsemen by the victory gained at Stamford Bridge, Yorkshire, in September, 1066. Hardly had the young king of the united English accomplished this momentous task when he was called upon to defend his country against the invasion of a new foe—the Normans led by that William who so soon was to become 'the Conqueror.' Harold had been preparing to resist William's threatened landing. The time had arrived, and when ready to march towards Hastings, he enters the headquarters of the army, where his officers are assembled, and issues the orders so picturesquely phrased by Tennyson (*Harold*, Act iv, Sc. 1)—

> *Set forth our golden Dragon, let him flap*
> *The wings that beat down Wales!*
> *Advance our standard of the Warrior,*
> *Dark among gems and gold; and thou, brave banner,*
> *Blaze like a night of fatal stars on those*
> *Who read their doom and die.*

Alas for the outcome of this brave boast!

But we have run somewhat ahead of the historic march of events. Long before the rise of Wessex to the control of all England, the 'Anglo-Saxon' settlers from northern parts of the continent had begun to cross the channel and recover from the barbarous Britons the fertile fields abandoned by the Romans. They brought with them many a wonder-story and superstition to add to the native stock and Celtic accretions,

among them the narrative of the exploits of that noble and
romantic Jutish hero Beowulf, who thus became an English
hero by adoption; but of him I shall speak more fully in the
next chapter. Hardly emerging from the legendary obscurity
of Beowulf and his time—say in the fifth century—one finds
traces of several other imported dragon-tales inherited from
remote Teutonic sources and more and more tinctured as the
centuries advanced with the theological notions and interpretations brought by early Christian missionaries to the British
people. Thus in *The Antiquary* (vol. 38, 1902) I find an account by E. Sidney Hartland of such a trace in Gloucestershire.

The church at Deerhurst in that county, he informs us, is
one of the oldest in western England; its tall square tower may
have "witnessed the Norman conquest, as it unquestionably
heard the clash of arms . . . on that bloody field by Tewkes-
bury." Two stones in the tower still bear some uncouth resemblance to the head of a mythical monster, and may be connected with a legend of a local dragon—"a serpent of prodigious bigness" that plagued the neighbourhood, poisoned the
inhabitants and slew their cattle. The people petitioned the
king, who offered a crown estate to anyone who should kill
the beast. This was achieved by John Smith, a blacksmith.
He put a large quantity of milk in a place frequented by the
monster; and the 'snake' having swallowed the whole "lay down
in the sun with his scales ruffled up," whereupon John advanced
and, by striking it between its scales with an ax, chopped off
its head. Mr. Hartland [31] believes that the protruding, jaw-like
figures set in the tower of this Deerhurst church have reference
to this legend; he refers to several similar carvings in continental churches that are known to commemorate the local deliverance of communities from dragon-rage. "One of the most

151

ordinary Anglo-Saxon sculptures," he remarks, "is that of a dragon. All sorts of Anglo-Celtic work bear this figure."

Scandinavians strengthened the general belief in reptiles as demons by inventing the theory of a great world-serpent, stories of which abound in the *Edda* and the sagas of old Norseland, and many evidences remain that this notion was well domesticated in Britain during the long domination of the 'Danes' in the north and east of that island. The 'Pollard Worm,' described so fully by Henderson is an example, although this demon was a wild boar—all such pests in the 'north countree' were 'worms'!—killed by a member of the Pollard family. A similar tradition belongs to Sockburn, and here the offender had the form of a serpent. Galloway has a legend of a snake which was accustomed to lie coiled around Mote Hill at Dalry —probably the site of an early Norman palisaded fort—a folk-tale outlined by Andrew Lang (*Academy,* Oct. 17, 1885) as follows:

The lord of Galloway offered a reward for its destruction; but one of his knights was swallowed up by the monster, horse and armor and all, and another was deterred by evil omens. The adventure was then attempted, as at Deerhurst, by a blacksmith, who devised a suit of armor for himself covered with long, sharp spikes, which could be drawn in or thrust out at the wearer's will. The snake of course swallowed him whole, like his predecessor, but as the smith slipped down his throat he suddenly shot out his spikes, and rolled about violently; nor did he cease until he had torn his way out through the monster's carcass!

This is not the only nor the earliest example of conquering the dragon from the inside: it was thought of hundreds of centuries before that. When Heracles undertook the deliverance of Hesione, daughter of Laomedon, king of Troy, from the sea-monster to which her father had exposed her, he sprang full-armed down the creature's gullet and hacked his way out of its maw. A similar folk-tale is related by Rumanian gypsies. One such story, indeed, has received ecclesiastical sanction to the extent, at least, of being incorporated in *The Golden Legend* and represented in stone among the sculptures adorning many European sacred edifices. The heroine here is that St. Margaret who was thrown into a dungeon after tortures of the kind that churchmen ascribe to their martyrs and have with equal piety and relish inflicted upon their opponents. "And whilst she was in prison she prayed our Lord," as Caxton recounts in his translation of *The Golden Legend,* "that the fiend that had fought with her He would visibly show unto her. And then appeared a horrible dragon and assailed her, and would have devoured her, but she made the sign of the cross and anon he vanished away. And in another place it is said that he swallowed her into his belly . . . and the belly broke asunder so she issued out all whole."

This miracle was denounced as apocryphal by critics centuries ago, yet the same set of adventures are related of Saints Martha, Veneranda, and Radegund. What troubled the minds of the monks was the difficulty of believing that the Devil had ever been killed! A ridiculous, but celebrated yarn of this class is that of the Lambton Worm, which I quote from the concise narrative by Hartland:

This was a creature caught by the heir of Lambton (in England on the banks of the Weir) one Sunday morning when fishing, and, to add to its iniquity, using very bad language.

He threw it into a well, where it grew and grew until it outgrew the well and resorted to the river, lying coiled by night thrice around a neighbouring hill. Meantime, the heir of Lambton, having repented of his evil life and spent seven years in the wars, returned, and determined to rid the land of the curse his wickedness had inflicted upon it. A wise woman whom he consulted advised him to get his suit of mail studded thickly with spearheads, and required him before going forth to the encounter to vow to slay the first living thing that met him on his way homeward, warning him that if he failed to perform the vow, no lord of Lambton for nine generations would die in his bed.

He met the worm and challenged it to the conflict by striking a blow on its head as it passed. It turned upon him and, winding its body around him, tried to crush him in its folds; but the spikes pierced it, and the closer its embrace the more deadly were the wounds it received, until with the flowing blood its strength ebbed away, and the knight with his good sword cut it in two.

The knight failed to fulfil his vow because his eager old father was the "first living thing met," and he could not bear to strike him down, so the curse remained on the Lambton family until worked out nine generations later by the death of Henry Lambton, M.P., in 1761.

Another and more burlesque comedy identified with a place and local families in England, and frequently spoken of, is that of The Dragon of Wantley. Its history is preserved in Bishop Percy's *Reliques* under the title—An Excellent Ballad of that most Dreadful COMBATE FOUGHT Between *Moore* of *Moore Hall,* and the Dragon of Wantley.

RAPHAEL'S 'ST. MARGARET SUBDUING THE EVIL BEAST.'
Italian, early sixteenth century.

This title-page bore also a picture of a scaly, lion-bodied monster "sharp, fierce and hungry-looking, with wings at his sides, an enormous tail, and two of his feet are hoofed, while the other two are strongly 'clawed'!" When the ballad was written is not known, but it refers to Sir Thomas Whortley, who aroused the hatred of the people by destroying a village on a hill at Wharncliffe in Yorkshire. He was a great aristocrat, serving as 'body-night' to Edward IV, Richard III, Henry VII, and Henry VIII, and died in 1514. He was vastly wealthy, jovial and hospitable, and was extravagantly fond of stag-hunting for which he kept a pack of hounds widely admired. Among his possessions was the village of Wantley, which gave him only partial satisfaction, for, as we read: "There were some freeholders within it with whom he wrangled and sued until he had beggared them and cast them out of their inheritance, and so the town was wholly his, which he pulled quite down and laid the buildings and town fields even as a common, wherein his main design was to keep deer, and make a lodge, to which he came at the time of the yere and lay there, taking great delight to hear the deer bell." Remains of this destroyed town were said to be visible not long ago on a lofty moor between Sheffield and Peristone, including the romantic cavity still known as the 'dragon's den,' and near it are a 'dragon's well' and a 'dragon's cellar.' The cruel and highhanded ejection of farmers, and destruction of good houses, just for sport, so disgusted and angered the people that they cast about for some means of redress. Near the castle of the wicked Whortley was Moore Hall (still standing), whose owner was far from friendly with the Whortleys. To the head of the Moore family, therefore, the distressed people went for a champion—

Sighing and sobbing, came to his lodging
And made a hideous noise.
Oh, save us all,
Moore of Moore Hall,
Thou peerless knight of the woods!
Do but slay this dragon—
He won't leave us a rag on—
We will give thee all our goods.

The champion refused the goods, but asked for

A fair maid of sixteen, that's brisk
And smiles about the mouth,

. . . . . .

To 'noint me o'er night ere I go to fight
And to dress me in the morning.

This is rather a reversal of the rescuing of maids customary in dragon-stories! The ballad—which is given in full in *The Reliquary* (vol. 18, London, 1878), and is discussed in Yorkshire local histories—relates the amazing combat in which the dragon was killed. Briefly, Moore, the doughty knight, clad in a suit of armour studded with long, sharp spikes, hid in a well to which the dragon was wont to come when thirsty; and when the beast arrived, and lowered its head into the well, Moore kicked it in the mouth, where alone it was vulnerable, and so accomplished its death. This method reminds us how, according to one account, Siegfried managed to kill the Nibelungen serpent Fafnir by hiding in a pit over which it must pass, and stabbing its belly as it crawled across the trench over the hero's head. In all these stories the dragon appears to be a wofully stupid and defenceless beast, agreeing with the foolish Devil of folklore.

It is probable that this Wantley ballad is founded on some incident of long-past feudal oppression, vengefully perpetuated by the Yorkshire peasantry by aid of this allegorical narrative —safer as a form of publication than would be an accusing statement in bald prose. Evictions of that sort have occurred far more recently than in the reputed era of the master of Wantley; and disagreements between neighbours still arise, leading third persons to take up arms in behalf of the oppressed, especially when the oppressor happens to be a rival or enemy of their own. So here was a nice dramatic situation ready to be turned into a pathetic (and saleable) ballad by some would-be-historical verse-maker clever enough to invent a 'dragon' to carry the somewhat dangerous burden of his song.

But the best of these legends, and one which carried nothing burlesque in the estimation of its hearers, or to the minds of those who now read its 'saga,' is the story of Beowulf. It is true that its scenes have not the background of British land-scape or habits; yet, as Bulfinch has said, "The splendid feat of Beowulf appeals to all English-speaking people in a very special way, since he is the one hero in whose story we may see the ideals of our English forefathers before they left their continental home."

Beowulf, a prince of the Greatas (probably a Swedish coast tribe, but possibly Jutes) gathered a band of dauntless vikings and sailed away to offer aid to Hrothgar, king of the Western Danes, who was in great distress because of the long-continued ravages of an unconquerable dragon—an allegory that seems to refer to certain historical happenings on the lower Rhine in the sixth century, A.D.

Grendel this monster grim was called,
   march-reiver mighty, in moorland living,
   in fen and fastness; fief of the giants
   the hapless wight a while had kept
   since the Creator his exile doomed.
On kin of Cain was the killing avenged
   by sovran God for slaughtered Abel. . . .
Of Cain awoke all that woful breed,
   etins and elves and evil spirits,
   as well as the giants that warred with God
   weary while.

The 'etins' mentioned here (Norse, *jotuns*) were giants, or ogres; and ancient tradition says they descended from the murderous Cain, whose progeny were thus cursed for his sin. This Grendel, whose home was in a great morass, is imagined as a nocturnal, man-eating monster in human form, with diabolical strength and ferocity. At frequent intervals he came in the night to Hrothgar's palace-hall, 'gold-bright Hereot,' where his Danish warriors slept, and seized, killed, and carried away as many men as he pleased as food for himself and his even more savage mother.

The Danes were cowed to powerlessness, and welcomed Beowulf and his band with a royal feast, where Beowulf declared his purpose to kill the giant, and to do it unarmed by wrestling-strength alone, boasting of past deeds of victory so obtained. The feast over, Hrothgar and his gracious queen retired to safer quarters, and the wine-bemused courtiers lay down to sleep on the benches and floor of the great hall. Grendel had knowledge of these doings, and gloating over the increased food supply, came that very night on one of his raids.

Bursting the 'forge-bolts' of the door with a blow of his fist, he seized, tore to pieces and devoured the first man he came to, then advanced upon another victim—the watchful Beowulf, who sprang up and clutched the cannibal's arm. Grendel tried to escape, but Beowulf held on:

> *The house resounded.*
> *Wonder it was the wine-hall firm*
> *in the strain of their struggle stood, to earth*
> *the fair house fell not.*

A hundred lines of the saga scarce suffice to tell of that prodigious, weaponless, struggle of hero against fiend; but at last Beowulf tears the giant's arm from its shoulder, and Grendel creeps away to die in the noisome fen. Great rejoicings and rewards follow, but the glorification is short-lived, for a few nights later Grendel's mother, burning with ferocious vengeance, murders in the midst of the slumbering Danes the King's favourite sage and warrior, and terror returns to the kingdom. Thereupon Beowulf prepares to finish the job by extinguishing this dam of a hellish brood. Sword in hand, this time, he marches to the 'horrid mere' where she hides, walks alone into its loathsome depths, and in a magical, submarine hall finds and destroys in a magical combat the last of the murderous tribe.

As this adventure was not the first so it was not to be the last of this righteous hero's battles with supernatural foes. Fifty years later Beowulf, now become a king in his own land, learns that in a certain part of his realm a fiery dragon—now not an anthropomorphic cannibal but an enormous serpent—has gone on the rampage. For three hundred years it had lain quiet in an antique stone grave, protecting there an immense treasure of heirlooms and coin "which some earl forgotten in ancient years, left the last of his lofty race, heedfully there had hidden away, dearest treasure." In hundreds of vivid verses we read what the old king was told, and how he goes forth to free his land from the rage of the fire-breathing dragon— majestic verse recounting an age-old legend of the guardian-dragon and utilizing it in a drama of heroism as Nordic bards conceived it in the height of its glory. One of the latest editors of this stirring epic summarizes and interprets this part of the narrative thus:

We have the old myth of a dragon who guards hidden treasure. But with this runs the story of some noble, last of his race, who hides all his wealth within this barrow and there chants his farewell to life's glories. After his death the dragon takes possession of the hoard and watches over it. A condemned or banished man, desperate, hides in the barrow, discovers the treasure, and while the dragon sleeps makes off with a golden beaker or the like, and carries it for propitiation to his master. The dragon discovers the loss and exacts fearful penalty from the people round about.

These burial-places of the inhabitants of western Europe, or of their chiefs, at least, known in Britain as barrows, and on the continent as dolmens, are small grave-chambers sunk in the ground and walled and roofed with stones; or, as in many cases, built on the surface of huge stone-slabs, the whole structure finally concealed beneath a mound of earth. Hundreds of such interments have been exposed by the washing away of the soil or by the sacrilege of robbers, as in the famous necropolis of Karnac in Brittany; and it is plain that many of them had a secret entrance into the tomb, as intimated in the poem. It was customary to bury with a great man not only his arms and accoutrements of war but often much or all of his wealth, and to try to render the sepulchre and its contents safe from molestation by publishing fearful curses and fictions about guardian spirits of frightful mien, usually clothed in dragon shape.

> *The fiery dragon*
> *fearful fiend, with flame was scorched.*
> *Reckoned by feet, it was fifty measures*
> *in length as it lay. Aloft erewhile*
> *it had revelled by night, and anon came back,*
> *seeking its den; now in death's sure clutch*
> *it had come to the end of its earth-hall joys.*
> *By it there stood the stoups and jars;*
> *dishes lay there, and dear-decked swords*
> *eaten with rust, as, on earth's lap resting,*
> *a thousand winters they had waited there.*
> *For all that heritage huge, that gold*
> *of bygone, was bound by a spell,*
> *so the treasure-hall could be touched by none*
> *of human kind.*

The robbery of graves filled with such treasures must have offered a strong temptation, and superstition surrounded the crime with every sort of danger. Lifting buried gold is still an uncanny business, and everywhere folklore teaches that its possession brings the worst of luck.

Old though he was, and feeble as compared with the strength that had torn Grendel's arm from its socket, King

Beowulf, despite the remonstrances of his court, goes against the poison-breathing, fire-belching 'worm'—that mighty serpent who nightly 'rages' through the burning grain-fields and at dawn retreats to his castle-like den in the barrow.   There Beowulf attacked the beast alone, bidding his followers stand away.   The battle was long and terrific, until finally one warrior, Wiglaf, could stand it no longer, but rushed to his sovereign's side, for Beowulf's sword had been broken by a too mighty stroke.

> *Then for the third time, thought on its feud,*
> *that folk-destroyer, fire-dread dragon,*
> *and rushed on the hero, where room allowed,*
> *battle-grim, burning; its bitter teeth*
> *closed on his neck, and covered him*
> *with waves of blood from his breast that welled.*

It was then Wiglaf reached the midst of the fray—

> *Heedless of harm, though his hand was burned,*
> *hardy-hearted, he helped his kinsman.*
> *A little lower the loathsome beast*
> *he smote with sword; his steel drove in*
> *bright and burnished; that blaze began*
> *to lose and lessen. At last the king*
> *wielded his wits again, war-knife drew,*
> *a biting blade by his breastplate hanging,*
> *and the Weders'-helm smote that worm asunder,*
> *felled the foe, flung forth its life.*

Here, as in many another tale of the period, where the dragon has the form of a serpent, victory is gained by the hero only when he is able with dagger or short sword to pierce the under side of the beast, where the belly and throat are unprotected by the tough scales that make its back and head invulnerable.

Beowulf's noble and unselfish fight for his people is his last. His wounds are fatal, and he dies; and the glittering wealth of gold and polished steel, so hardly won, are buried with him in that royal tomb whose site no man knows.

Chapter Fourteen

THE DRAGON AND THE HOLY CROSS

IT IS noticeable in scanning the legends thus far recited, as purposely grouped, that the supernatural apparitions described, requiring superhuman feats for their extermination, were killed off because they were destroying human life and property, particularly cattle, or possessed desired treasures; not, as in the East, because they were maliciously withholding rain or other needed waters; and nowhere in Britain or northern Europe have we encountered a captive maiden or one about to be sacrificed to a dragon, which is the ruling feature in another and more recent group of tales. This, it seems to me, betokens a distinctly northern attitude of mind, and indicates legendary descent through a history of migrations from Scythia (to go no farther east for origins), where women were little regarded as compared with property, and chivalric sentiment all but absent from men's minds.

The type of stories, on the other hand, which was derived from aboriginal Greek imaginings, more or less tinctured with Hebrew and Egyptian teaching, and which filtered westward along the European shore of the Mediterranean, south of the great mountains dividing that sea from the basin of the Baltic, included almost always the idea of rescuing a woman in danger, and represent a southern as distinct from a northern inspiration and dramatic sense. Dr. Spence has remarked that the mediæ-

164

val dragon was a story teller's, or literary, subterfuge to give the hero an opportunity to be heroic. This latter style in dragon-stories remains to be treated; but before proceeding to that I want to say something about those tales current in Roman times and for centuries afterward on the continent of Europe, as recorded with pious credulity in the biographies of Catholic saints. These zealous missionaries, who went forth from Rome to spread the gospel of Christ beyond the Alps, often at the risk of life (the hardships endured by missionary priests among Canadian Indians in the eighteenth century make us understand what must have been the experience of many a would-be teacher among the wild tribes of northern Europe), were men who believed in a real, and at will corporeal, Satan and his imps; and they felt themselves obstructed by powers of darkness quite as much as by the natural reluctance of the 'savages' to abandon their ancestral gods and fetishes—in fact the apostles regarded such reluctance as due to past instruction as well as to present advice by the Devil. From the serpent who tempted Eve in the Garden of Eden, down to the fire-breathing all-devastating dragon (Greek *drako,* English 'drake,' literally 'big snake') of *Revelation,* the missionaries had the authority of the Scriptures to make it the image and synonym of Satan; and it was easy to impress this image upon the minds of pupils of the new faith, terrified by pictures of the tortures awaiting their souls at the hands of this same clawed and horned devil-dragon unless they came into the Roman religious fold. Remembering these threats, and recalling the clerical faith of the time in the divinely endowed virtue of the Cross or its symbols, and the miracle-working powers imparted by its aid to 'holy men,' there need be no wonder at the monkish legends recorded with such sincerity by the early chroniclers.

The industry of Dr. E. Cobham Brewer has brought together, in his *Dictionary of Miracles,* a large number of such records, culled from the authentic writings of St. Jerome, Gregory of Tours, and other fathers of the Church, among which is the following characteristic example indited by Richard de la Val d'Isère, the successor of the 'great' St. Bernard of Menthon (993–1008), who declares he was an eye-witness of the incident. "Saint Bernard left at the bottom of the Alps," as Dr. Brewer repeats the story, "the bishop, clergy and procession, which had followed him thither; and with nine pilgrims ascended the mountain where was the brigand Procus, called 'the giant,' and worshipped as a god. Saint Bernard and his companions came up to the giant and saw hard by a huge dragon ready to devour them. Bernard made the sign of the Cross, and then threw his stole over the monster's neck. The stole instantly changed itself into an iron chain, except the two ends held in the saint's hands." The nine pilgrims thereupon killed the dragon, and the two silken ends of the stole were long preserved in the abbey of St. Maurice-en-Valais.

This method of subduing Satanic demons which, owing to the ancient curse (*Genesis* 3:14) were obliged to assume a form that compelled them to crawl on their bellies, was a favourite one—we have already seen it used by St. Samson in Ireland. St. Germanus (fifth century) marched boldly into the dark cavern in Scotland inhabited by a prodigious dragon, threw his handkerchief around its neck, and led it forth to a deep pit into which he cast it, and so relieved the district of a man-killing nuisance. Paris was freed from a dreadful dragon of goulish habits in A.D. 136, by St. Marcel, who knocked it on the head three times with his cross. This done he wrapped his cloak about the creature's neck and led it four miles beyond

166

the city's gates, where it was set free after it had promised to remain in a certain wood to the end of time—at any rate it has never reappeared. This is told by Gregory of Tours. After Ste. Marthe had quieted the frightful dragon of the Rhône, she conducted it by her girdle (Maury describes it more piquantly as her garter) to Tarascon, where the people put it to death; and they have been celebrating this deliverance ever since. Several other saintly heroes made captives of cave-dwelling monsters by similarly sanctified leading-strings.

In another class of cases evil beasts, and particularly serpents, are subjugated by holy men by the exhibition of a crucifix or some sign representing it. A terrorized community would summon a saint, sometimes from abroad, to deliver it from a ·despoiling monster (in one instance with a penchant for devouring children—possibly a reminiscence of child sacrifice to bloody deities) just as villagers in India or Africa now seek the help of sportsmen to kill for them a man-eating lion or tiger.

Out of these stories and faiths came the ascription to many of the religious worthies of the Middle Ages of a dragon in some form as a badge of distinction—needful when the mass of the people could not read, and must have some means of identifying the 'saints' one from another, just as they had to have a bush to tell them where wine was sold and a bloody pole instead of a written sign to indicate the barber's shop. In his book, *Saints and Their Emblems,* M. M. Drake shows that dragons appear thirty-five times attached to thirty martyrs and other persons, for some exhibit more than one, perhaps having more than a single experience with the fearsome beast. The artist depicting the saint in statue, painting or decorated glass, tries also to tell the story attached to his or her name.

Thus in the case of Martha of Bethany she is shown in a sixteenth century window at St. Mary's in Shrewsbury, England, holding an asperge and holy water vessel with a dragon behind her; but elsewhere you may see her more often in the attitude of vanquishing a dragon by presenting her crucifix to his gaze. Instances might be multiplied, but the reader may find them in the *Catalogues* and descriptive *Lives* of mediæval celebrities of the Church.

Maury [32] connects the many tales of the freeing of various districts of serpents with the Biblical promise: "They shall take up serpents . . . and it shall not hurt them" (*Mark* 16:18). Thus is explained St. Paul's escape from harm by the adder which he flung into the fire in Malta. Hence arose the popular belief that the ministers of the gospel were immune from poisoning by the venom of serpents and might safely attack them. "In Brittany," Maury reminds us, "the apostles who reached the faith are regarded as having destroyed serpents that ravaged the country. Thus did St. Cadon [at Karnac], St. Naudet and St. Pol de Léon [at Batz]. In Gaul in the fifth century St. Keyna the Virgin destroyed the snakes that ravaged the country in the vicinity of Keysham. In Pomerania were expelled serpents that vomited flames." St. Radegond fought in Poictiers the dragon called Grand Gueule; St. Clement did a like service at Metz; St. Saturnin at Bernay; St. Armond at Maestricht, etc.; and some of these Christians are reported to have been snake-bitten without injury to their health. The most famous, however, of all these exploits is that by St. Patrick in Ireland, and it is more manifestly mythical than any of the others because *there never were* any snakes in Erin's Isle! A sequel to this beloved tradition is less familiar than the main facts, and is told by Dr. Brewer as follows:

ST. MICHAEL.
Italian, fifteenth century.

ST. GEORGE.
German, late fifteenth
century.

Courtesy of the Metropolitan Museum.

When St. Patrick ordered the serpents of Ireland into the sea one of the older reptiles refused to obey; but the saint over-mastered it by stratagem. He made a box and invited the serpent to enter in, pretending it would be a nice place for it to sleep in. The serpent said the box was too small, but St. Patrick maintained it was quite large enough. So high at length rose the argument that the serpent got into the box to prove it too small; whereupon St. Patrick clapped down the lid and threw the box into the sea.

Critics justly regard most of these tales as allegories of the success had by various missionary priests in slaying the 'devils' of paganism or of false doctrine in their several fields of labour, and in converting local groups of people to Christianity. Some such expulsion of native rites and idols from one or another district probably indicates the reality behind the many legends of serpent clearance. Several of these tales, nevertheless, seem to me based upon actual feats of heroism, as, for example, that exploit of Bishop Romanus, annually celebrated at Rouen, which may not be wholly mythical, since the 'horrible dragon' in this case might well be a bad man instead of a false doctrine. The adventure of that soldier-general of the army of Licenus in Thrace of the fourth century, who fought and slaughtered a dragon with his sword, and after afterward canonized as St. Theodorus of Heraclea, furnishes another case. The Thracians would probably insist, could they return to tell us about it, that Licenus and his officers had put something to the sword more strategic than dragons, and more substantial than heresy.

These few typical examples out of many may suffice to show the way in which the general belief in supernatural and more or less harmful beings was utilized by the early Christian

169

missionaries in Europe, to impress the sanctions of the new religion upon both the heathen and the indifferent or hostile men and women to whom they preached. Some of the best remembered of these legendary incidents, involving acts of extraordinary heroism or religious significance, have been periodically celebrated by quasi-religious ceremonies in Europe until recent times.

The most serious, elaborate, and picturesque of these festivals is that which, until lately, was annually celebrated at the ancient town of Tarascon, in Provence. It commemorated the taming of a singularly horrible and ravenous demon-beast by Ste. Marthe; but just who she was no one knows. Some say her name is a Christianized form of that of the Phœnician goddess Martis, patroness of sailors, whose symbols were a ship and a dragon; others recall classic reminiscences of Hercules and his battling with local giants, one of which was named Taras or Tariskos. Baring-Gould [33] investigated the matter at length, and concluded that a Christian woman-missionary called Martha, who, soon after the death of Jesus, came with others to this part of Gaul, has become strangely confused with a Syrian prophetess named Martha, who accompanied the Roman general Gaius Marius, and aided him greatly by her magic and inspiration, during the two years of hard fighting by which he beat back the ravaging hordes of northern barbarians who invaded southern Gaul at the end of the second century, B.C. He regards the 'dragon' in this case as an image of the undying recollection of the appalling terror, devastation and suffering wrought by that invasion, and the ceremony as a grateful acknowledgment of the deliverance. The citizens generally, however, know little and care less about these explanations, for their minds are fixed on the miracle by which their forefathers

170

were rescued. Roman monuments remaining at or near Tarascon, which represent Marius, Julia his wife, and the Syrian
woman, the people have interpreted for centuries past as figures of Lazarus, Mary Magdalen, and Martha the hostess of
Jesus. The legendary incident celebrated is this:

While Martha was preaching Christianity to the pagan
people at Arles an urgent message was sent to her from Tarascon, reciting that an awful dragon called the *Tarasque,* whose
lair was in the neighbouring desert of Crau, was killing the
Tarasconais, and they begged her to come and destroy it. She
gladly complied, and going to his cave was able, by sheer force
of lovingness (and a sprinkler of holy water), to subdue and
regenerate the ravaging *Tarasque,* so that he meekly followed
her into the midst of the astonished populace. "Along the
bright ways of the city," as the legend goes, "the procession
moved: a crowd of excited people, a beautiful woman with
the light playing round her head, leading by a silken cord a
reformed monster who ambles after her as quietly as if he
were a pet lamb. . . . And never again did he ravage the
country or carry off so much as a single babe after Ste. Marthe
had pointed out to him, with her usual sweet reasonableness,
how wrong-headed and how essentially immoral such conduct
had been." So Mona Caird [34] pictures the scene of the deliverance from a devouring creature more dreadful, if we can
credit mediæval descriptions, than anything we have thus far
discovered in this history of beastly demons—a figure worthy
to represent the hellish character of the Teutonic invasion of
this fair land 2000 years ago.

Toward the end of the fifteenth century, the kindly and
artistic king René, desiring to gratify and amuse his favourite
subjects, the Tarasconais, instituted a fête, the central feature

to be a representation of the legendary miracle for the glory of Ste. Marthe. It was appointed for April 14, 1474, and proved a lasting success, for it was repeated annually up to the beginning of this the twentieth century. "A grotesquely terrible monster, red and black, of the pantomime type, made of wood, paraded the streets on the second Sunday after Pentecost. Enormous red-rimmed eyes stared out of a round, catlike countenance fringed with bristling white whiskers. The men inside who carried him, and whose legs were his, danced and capered about, so as to make the huge wooden tail wag and upset any spectator whose curiosity prompted him to come too near. For it was the monster's day out. His ferocity was as yet untamed. Then the *Tarasque* was taken back to the stable, where he is still to be seen, to await the day of his doom, St. Martha's day, 29th July. Tamed now, and gentle as a sucking dove, he was led forth once more, but this time by a ribbon held by a young girl, as a lamb to the slaughter."

Although this pantomime was attended by clergy who endeavoured to make it impressive, the day was one of hilarity and fun of every sort; and the gay crowd sang as they followed the lumbering figure through the streets the chant that they say King René himself wrote—

> *Lagadigaddeu!*
> *La Tarasco!*
> *Lagadigaddeu!*
> *La Tarasco!*
> *De casteu!*
> *Leissas-la passa*
> *La vieio masco!*
> *Leissas-la passa*
> *Que vai dansa!, etc.*

Another long-lived fête sanctioned by the Church is that of the 'Privilege' in Rouen. In that historic city on the Seine a narrow street leads down from the cathedral to the river, crossing on its way a large open space where stands the Chapelle de la Fierté Saint-Romain. With this ancient chapel is connected a curious custom, which was exercised for more than 750 years. The charter establishing it was granted to the Chapter of Rouen Cathedral by King Dagobert in the eighth century, and empowered the archbishop to release, once every year on Ascension Day, a chosen criminal from among those in the city condemned to death. On every Ascension Day, therefore, the people of Rouen flocked into the streets to witness the ceremonies with which this behest was carried out—the Procession of the Privilege of Saint Romain. First came the solemn visit of the Church to the Civic authorities, carrying the annual formal proclamation of the privilege (*fierté*). "Then every prison in the city must be searched, and every prisoner put on oath and examined as to the cause of his imprisonment. Finally the election of the favoured prisoner was put to vote of the Chapter. . . . He then confessed to the Chapter of Saint Romain, his fetters were removed, and he followed the archbishop to the Place Haute-Vielle Tour, where, in the Chapelle de la Fierté, a solemn service made him a free man. A solemn and magnificent procession then bore him, crowned with flowers, to the great thanksgiving Mass, after which he was free to go whither he would."

So the Marshalls[35] describe the ceremony in their volume on the cathedral cities of France; and they give in the subjoined paragraph the legend that accounts for its origin, explaining that this legend appears to be of later date than the festival, which is mentioned "certainly as late as the twelfth century, and continued to delight the Rouennais as late as 1790." It looks to me as if it originated as an ingenious method by some kindly Church authority, in a time when tyranny ruled rather than law and justice, and innocent men, or personal enemies, might be immured in dungeons and forgotten, to make an an-

THE GARGOUILLE OF ROUEN.

From the stained-glass window in the cathedral at Rouen.

nual survey and clearance of the prisons, freeing persons unjustly confined. This is the legend:

While Romain was bishop of Rouen a terrible dragon laid waste all the land and devoured the inhabitants. No one dared approach the monster, who was known as the Gargoyle [gargouille] until Saint Romain, armed only with his sanctity, set out to subdue it, accompanied by a condemned criminal—the prototype of those who were released on Holy Thursday—when

174

*the Gargoyle at once submitted and, with the episcopal stole
around its neck, was led by the prisoner to the water's edge.
[It was then pushed in and drowned, whereupon the 'condemned criminal' was presumably rewarded for his courage by
being given his freedom.] At the head of the Portail de la
Calende, the north porch of the cathedral, stands the figure of
Saint Romain, and under his feet, with the stole around his
neck, is the Gargoyle, craning its head around to look into the
face of the bishop with the expression of a very hideous but
very faithful dog. . . . In memory of the occurrence the standard of the dragon was borne in the processions at the Privilege
—banners similar to those of the dragons of Bayeux and Salis-
bury.*

Similar festivals and processions in which the dragon, as a
symbol of wickedness, heresy, and so forth, took place in old
days in many European communities. We read of them at
Metz, where the evil beast was dubbed *Grauly,* at Bergerac
(the dragon of St. Front), at the abbey of Fleury, and even
in Paris. "The images are made of silk, very large, and are
manœuvred by children hidden in the interior." The celebra-
tions were commonly identified with the Rogation days, and
some have continued up to fairly modern times. Rogation
days, as set apart by the Catholic Church, are the three days
preceding Ascension Day, which is the fortieth day after Easter;
and they are observed with prescribed litanies or liturgical prayers, and in some places with public processions, all the ceremonies combining to make a supplication for God's blessing
on the crops. In view of this purpose, and the spring season,
it is very significant that the dragon should be associated with
this particular celebration—a prayer for rain! Mr. J. W. Legg

175

contributed some statements as to these ceremonies to *Notes and Queries* for October, 1857, which are condensed below:

In the thirteenth century inventory of 'ornaments' of Old Sarum cathedral banners called Leo and Draco are specified. Documents state that at that epoch the use of these banners was ordained in certain rubrics, e.g., for Rogation processions. The custom of carrying images of the dragon is spoken of by many liturgical writers. Besides the figure in the Old Sarum Processionale, *Barrault and Martin give a drawing of a processional dragon preserved at Metz at page 44 of their* Baton Pastoral *(Paris, 1856). Sometimes the dragon was carried on Palm Sunday, as at Orléans, when both a dragon and a cock, as well as these banners, were borne. I think these banners must be separated from the Easter dragon. The latter was a serpent-shaped candlestick for the triple candle, which was carried at Rouen on Easter Eve until the end of the seventeenth century. The processional dragon is not peculiar to either Sarum or the Celtic church. What its source is, whether a figure of the noisome beasts to which St. Mamertus began the Rogations, or whether it has come from the* labarum *of Constantine, or is of Pagan origin, I must leave others to determine.*

Maury records that at Provins, in France, the bell-ringers of the churches formerly bore in Rogations processions, in advance of the Cross, an image of a winged dragon, and also an image of a lizard, garnished with flowers, in memory of ravenous beasts. At Paris the dragon always carried at Rogations was regarded as the image of the monster exterminated by Saint Marcel. At Aix-en-Provence, the marchers saw arranged upon an eminence called Dragon Rock, near a chapel dedicated to

St. Andrew, the figure of a dragon in imitation of the one tradition said that apostle had killed.

A curious survival of these mediæval combinations of piety and pranks was the 'snap-dragon' as a feature in the festive procession accompanying the induction of every new mayor in Norwich, England, up to 1832. Here the image was small enough to be managed by one man inside; it had a distensible neck so that the head could be wagged about, short, batlike wings, and a pig's tail. As described and pictured in an old number of *Harper's Magazine*, the head had its lower jaw furnished with a plate of iron "garnished with enormous nails which produced a terrible clatter." The jaws were made to open and shut by means of strings, and as the creature marched along, its head turning to right and left, the children amused themselves by throwing halfpence into the gaping jaws.

It must be borne in mind, of course, that the word 'dragon' in these mediæval narratives does not necessarily imply that the creature for which it stands had a snake-like or crocodilian form, for the ghost-haunted minds of the people of that era readily conjured up marvellous and abominable shapes and combinations of animals with which no legitimate and self-respecting dragon would consent to associate, even in the limbo betwixt fable and allegory. Fine examples of the weird and unholy extravagances possible to a brisk imagination set at work to devise vivid caricatures of beastly demons may be found in Albrecht Dürer's etched illustrations for the Faust legend, the temptation of St. Anthony, etc.; but three thousand years before him similar monstrosities were cut in miniature by the gem-engravers of Crete on seals and ornaments. Dürer never saw these little horrors, which perhaps were intended to be talismans to ward off evil glances; but when he was bidden to depict the grizzly terrors that seemed to swarm about the sorely abused mind and body of the half-starved eremite in his chilly cell, his fancy could reach no other result than that found by the Ægean artist so long ago. "The Dream," painted by Raphael, is another collection of horrors of unnatural history. It is in and by art, indeed, that the fiction we are considering has been preserved to us; and artists now tell us that the survival and extensive use of the dragon in art is accounted for by its 'manageability' as an element in a decorative composition. All the multitude of dragon-forms, diverse as they are in reflecting the fears or the fancies of widely differing races of men, agree in fulfilling certain conditions that make them exceedingly useful in ornamentation. It is of course always possible to put some animal figure in place of a dragon, but the real creature is not nearly so manageable as the imaginary one. "The actual creature, whatever it may be," explains the English artist Lewis F. Day, "must be considered to some extent from the point of view of nature; but the monster leaves the artist free. . . . This is an incalculable convenience in design, and enables the artist to arrive with certainty at the effect at which he aims. There is a kind of keeping, too, between the ideal creature and the ideal ornament. The natural birds and other living creatures that occur at intervals among the purely ornamental arabesques of the *cinque-cento* always seem to me out of place. They suggest that the artist was not quite content with his art of ornament, and must needs relieve himself at intervals by indulging in a bit of naturalism. . . . If, then, the dragon has lingered in art long past the time when we have any faith in him, it will be seen that there is a reason for his prolonged existence."

Since the blazonry of more or less boastful badges on

knights' shields and family possessions began, the dragon, as 'wivern,' has been a favourite device in European heraldry, and possibly the most antique one. Long before any College of Heralds was instituted we learn by tradition of the helmet-crests of the heroes of Romance. Tennyson sings of the 'great Pendragonship' and that sightly helm of Arthur, "to which for crest the golden dragon clung."

Let me quote another pertinent paragraph from Mr. Day's fine article in the third volume (1880) of the *Magazine of Art*:

The heraldic dragon conforms, after the manner of its kind, to decorative necessities. His business is to look full of energy and angry power. His jaws are wide; his claws are sharp; wings add to his speed and to his terrors; he is clothed with scaly and impenetrable armour, and he lashes his tail in fury; and all the while he is careful to spread himself out on shield or banner that all his powers may be displayed. In the days before the invention of the term 'fine art' the dragon was frequently introduced into pictures of sacred and legendary subjects, and it invariably formed an ornamental feature in the composition. St. Michael and St. George were habitually triumphant over the evil thing; and . . . if the rigid virtues were sometimes insipid, it must be allowed that the demons were usually grotesquely characteristic and often delightful in colour. The grim humour of the mediæval Germans found its latest exponent in Albert Durer, some of whose imaginary creations are very remarkable. . . . They belong half to Gothic tradition and half to Renaissance influence, but yet they are wholly German and wholly Dureresque. The creatures of the Italian cinque-cento partook for the most part of the grace of the ornaments of which they were a part, though occasionally

179

there lurks among the beautiful and fanciful foliation a monster that is inexpressibly loathsome. Art might well dispense with such imaginings. If the fabled creature is to live in ornament —and why should it not?—let it be on the supposition that it is a thing of beauty.

Chapter Fifteen

TO THE GLORY OF SAINT GEORGE

THE WESTERN half of our history is closing true to form—a history that originated in myth and resulted in the loftiest reality. It began in the romantic fable of Perseus and Andromeda, and it ends on the shore of the Western Ocean to the glory of Saint George and Merrie England!

The connecting lineage and record are clear. The Hero family has been a prolific one, and widely spread, with a history full of noble diversity, but its temper has held true, and its mission of the rescue of maidens in peril, or, more largely, of distressed and wrong-headed peoples, has never been neglected: its career is a continuous picture of the ideal of the West—knightly valour in service, the duty of the strong to aid the weak. From Persia to Italy, from cultured Greece to the barbarous shore of the Atlantic, the tale of noble deeds was told, the fame of one and another brave soul was celebrated, and so Chivalry was born of Romance, and the Renaissance arose to rejuvenate a benighted old world.

Whether or not the names we read were ever or never those of actual men; whether or not anything like a dragon ever threatened forlorn princesses or devastated a smiling countryside, is of no consequence. As history, and its record may be as unsubstantial as the quickly dissolving clouds that reflected a rosy light upon the towers of a mythical Ilium—doubtless it

181

is, for the most part, only an immortal legend repeating itself as do human generations, but it portrays, century after century, the highest virtue in the manly soul.

It is needless to spend time over the variants in what we may style the Perseus legend as written in classic and mediæval books and poems. Stories identical in substance with that of the rescue of Andromeda from the jaws of a monster were widely related in antiquity and have not yet been forgotten. They form a class by themselves, differentiated from the traditions and fables that have heretofore been related, by the fact that always a young virgin, usually of royal birth, is delivered from impending death by a bold and ardent youth; and that in most cases there is the attendant, but less important, fact that the hero is nearly robbed of his just reward (the maiden's hand and heart) by the evil machinations of a rival who never quite succeeds. A typical example is found in far Arabia. One day, as we are told, a dragon comes to a city in Yemen and demands a beautiful virgin. The lot falls on the king's daughter, but a young knight kills the monster, and the brave adventurer gets the girl. Another very old example is that attached to the most precious relic in the storied island of Rhodes. Luke the Evangelist, the islanders say, desired to move the body of John the Baptist from its burial-place in Cæsarea to Antioch, but was able to transfer only the saint's right hand, with which Jesus had been baptized. "Subsequently it was deposited in the new Hagia Sophia at Constantinople, and after further adventures reached security in Rhodes. While it yet remained in Antioch a dragon haunted the country about that city, and the people appeased the monster yearly with the sacrifice of one of their number, chosen by lot. At last the lot fell on a maid whose father greatly venerated the holy relic.

182

DÜRER'S 'ST. GEORGE AND THE DRAGON.'
German woodcut, early sixteenth century.

183

Making as though he would kiss the hand, he bit off a fragment from the thumb: and when his daughter was led out to sacrifice he cast this fragment into the dragon's jaws and the monster quickly choked and perished."

A widely familiar 'St. George' legend is that belonging to Mansfield, in Germany, over whose church-door is a statue commemorating the incident. The great man of the place at the time was Count Mansfield, and near the town is a hill still called Lindberg because in former days it was the abode of a *lindwurm*, or dragon, to which the townspeople were obliged to give a young woman every day. Soon no more maidens were to be found except the knight's own daughter. Whereupon Count Mansfield rode forth and slew the beast, and the citizens made him a 'saint' and gave him (or somebody else!) a statue, in spite of his previous indifference as to the fate of *their* daughters. Mansfield is one of the many places believed locally to be the site of the famous combat of that 'St. George' whose exploits were as numerous and widespread as were those of Hercules—in each case probably a misplaced tradition of some dimly remembered fight between local barons or bullies.

A still closer approximation to the Perseus type was taken down a few years ago from the lips of an illiterate peasant woman of the Val d'Arno, Italy, and is quoted by Hartland. A part of it describes the hero finding in a seaside chapel a lovely maiden, who urges him to hasten on his way lest he suffer the fate to which she is doomed, namely, to be eaten by a seven-headed dragon. Instead of obeying her he dismounts, attacks the dragon on its rising from the sea, and cuts out its seven tongues which he carries away—these trophies proving his claim, a few months later, to the credit of the feat and the hand of the willing girl.

184

This seven-headed, seven-tongued hydra-dragon of fiction appears all down the ages, at least since the days of Hercules. Such a brute, to which a king's daughter is to be offered, figures in Grimm's tale of The Two Brothers, and variants may be found in folk-legends everywhere in Europe. That within comparatively recent times it was popularly believed to be a reality is shown by serious accounts of its doings in books regarded as sensible and authoritative. Conrad Gesner gives a picture in his *Historia Animalium* of a hydra in the form of a serpent, "the heads like those of lions and as it were ornamented with crowns, two feet in the front of the body, the tail twisted inwards." He relates that this hideous, aquatic creature was brought from Turkey to Venice in the year 1530, exposed to public view, and afterward sent to the king of France. The Italian compiler Aldrovandus, a contemporary, illustrates in his book about serpents a seven-headed dragon; and in the *Encyclopædia Londonensis,* issued in 1755, may be seen a large coloured plate of a dreadful, seven-headed creature credited to Seba, an author who published a *Thesaurus* of natural history about 1750, with an extensive account of it.

And so at last we come to our own Saint George! Who was this patron of the valorous, this model of devotion to an ideal of duty, this indomitable George? Nobody knows. He has been relegated to the sun-myths, and declared a mere relic of Mithraism. Gibbon and others identified him with the author of Arianism, but Eastern churches were named for the martyr before that prelate existed. It has also been said that he was that nameless Christian who tore down the edict of persecution in Nicomedia. These and other identifications have been discarded. The nearest approach to probability that any distinct personality is at the root of this heroic development of a noble idealism lies in a tradition that a Christian man named George (or its equivalent) was martyred in Palestine before the era of Constantine the Great; that he became the object of a religious cult (said to be referred to in an inscription dated A.D. 367); and that in 1868 his sepulchre was discovered at Lydda (or Diospolis) near Jerusalem, where his martyrdom is alleged to have occurred. Tradition has expanded these facts (if they be facts) into a story in many varying versions, the most acceptable summary of which appears to be the following:

"According to legend [this Christian George] was born, about A.D. 285, of noble parents in Cappadocia, eastern Anatolia. As he grew to manhood he became a soldier; his courage in battle soon won him promotion, and he was attached to the personal staff of the emperor Diocletian. When this ruler decided to enter on his campaign of persecution, George resigned his commission and bitterly complained to the emperor. He was immediately arrested, and when promises failed to make him change his mind he was tortured with great cruelty. . . . At last he was taken to the outskirts of the city and beheaded [April 23, A.D. 303]. . . . The earliest narrative of his martyrdom known to us is full of the most extravagant marvels: three times George is put to death, chopped into small pieces, buried deep in the earth, and consumed by fire, but each time he is resuscitated by God. Besides this we have dead men brought to life to be baptized, wholesale conversions, including that of the 'Empress Alexandra,' armies and idols destroyed simultaneously, beams of timber suddenly bursting into leaf, and finally milk flowing instead of blood from the martyr's severed head."

This and several other more or less extravagant, and equally legendary accounts derived from old manuscripts and books, are related and discussed extensively in Mrs. Cornelia S. Hulst's [36] admirable history of this essentially mythical saint or hero, and his veneration in Europe.

This was a remarkable man, whoever and whatever he was, and it is not surprising that, probably stimulated by some shining circumstance unknown to us, he became so distinguished in the religious world of his time. Besides St. Stephen, he is the only martyr venerated by the entire Church; is one of the fourteen 'great martyrs' and 'trophy-bearers' of the Greek Church, and is honoured by special masses and ceremonies in the Latin, Syrian, and Coptic communions. All over the Orient, in Greece, Italy and Sicily, many churches were dedicated to him in the sixth century, and since. His relics are scattered over the entire Church, Santo Georgio in Velabro, at Rome, possessing the head. Holweck [37] catalogues this saint's ecclesiastical distinctions thus: "S. George is principal patron of England, Catalaunia (Spain), Liguria (Italy), Aragon, Georgia, Modena, Farrara (24 April), of the isle of Syros, dioceses of Wilna, Limburg, Regio de Calabria, and other dioceses, also of the Teutonic Knights, minor patron of Portugal, Lithuania, Constantinople. He is protector of soldiers, archers, knights, saddlers, sword-cutlers, and of horses, against fever, etc. He is mentioned daily in the Greek mass." Moslems, in fact, reverence Saint George, identifying him with the Prophet Elijah, and have long allowed Christians to celebrate a mass once a year at the tomb of the martyr at Lydda, in Palestine, now a mosque; and the first church dedicated to St. George (at Zarava, in Hauran, A.D. 514) was a re-consecrated mosque.

That the fame of this martyr had spread in very early times to Britain is shown by references to him in the writings of the

Venerable Bede and in other chronicles. Ashmole says, in his history of the Order of the Garter, that King Arthur placed a picture of St. George on his banners, and Selden states that he was regarded as the patron-saint of England in Saxon times. It was not, however, until after the great Third Crusade, in which the English played the leading part, led by their magnificent prince, Richard the Lion-hearted, that George, as warrior rather than as martyr, became noticeable in that national dignity. It was believed among the disheartened crusaders before Acre that St. George had appeared to Richard in a vision and had encouraged him to continue the long and dreadful siege; and afterward the story spread that the troops themselves had beheld him, on a white horse, fighting for them above their heads in the drifting smoke of battle, as did the angel who was "captain of the hosts of the Lord" when Joshua was battling against the walls of Jericho. Even the French soldiers under Robert, son of William the Conqueror, accepted him as their patron and defender.

It is perhaps to this figure that Dr. Hanauer [38] refers in relating this bit of folklore current in Palestine. A fountain (Gihon?) in the outskirts of Jerusalem was formerly a part of the water-supply of the city, but a big dragon took possession of it and demanded a youth or maid every time anyone came for water; until at last, as usual, only the king's daughter was left. When she was about to be sent, Mar Jirys appeared in golden panoply mounted on a white steed, and riding full tilt at the dragon, he pierced it dead between the eyes. This is probably the same spring which is noted for its intermittent flow, which the people explain by saying that the dragon drinks the water low whenever it wakes, and when the beast sleeps the water rises. The Tyrolese speak of a dragon that "eats

BOXWOOD CARVING OF ST. GEORGE.

Germany, fifteenth century. Courtesy of the Metropolitan
Museum.

its way out of the rock" when the intermittent spring at Bella, in Krain, begins to flow. The Maltese also have a dragon's spring which issues from a cavern with noises said to be the snorts of the monster within its source.

The returning crusaders, reporting this supernatural assistance in full faith, made a very deep impression on the credulous populace of England, who at once proclaimed this White Knight military protector of the kingdom; and in 1222 the Council of Oxford ordained that the feast day of St. George (April 23) should be observed as a minor holy day in the English Church. In 1330 he was formally adopted as the patron-saint of the Order of the Garter just then instituted by Edward III, which was equivalent to an ascription for the whole country, and he became that indeed when the Royal Chapel at Windsor was dedicated to him in 1348. He was invoked by Henry V at Agincourt (1415), where the English swept forward to victory with the inspiring battle-cry of his name.

> *Saint George he was for England,*
> *Saint Denis was for France,*

rings out the old song!

Thus this hero of the Middle Ages became in England more than elsewhere the favourite of the people and the principal figure of the time in mystic plays, mummeries, and religious dramas and processions, especially on Corpus Christi Day. Until recent times one of the diversions in Wiltshire and other English counties was the play "St. George and Turkey-Snipe" (a corruption of Turkish Knight), wherein a Christian knight overcomes a Saracen. The opening words of this pious drama are quoted by Miss Urlin as follows:

I am King George, the noble champion bold,
And with my trusty sword I won ten thousand pounds in gold.
It was I that fought the fiery Dragon, and brought him to the
slaughter,—
And by these means I won the king of Egypt's daughter.

It is not surprising that mistakes and legends early began
to cluster around this notable character all over the continent.

Legends are the weeds of history. They are sown by winds
of gossip, and bear fruits of the imagination which sometimes
are sweet and wholesome but are more often ugly and baneful.
They take deep root and flourish prodigiously, overshadowing
the less interesting growths of fact and voucher, and obscuring,
by a sort of protective mimicry, the truths in tradition. For
example: where, if anywhere, among the many places, do the
red flowers growing year by year on this and that meadow or
hilltop, indicate the *true* spot "where the Dragon was killed"?
Here and there we may say—as at Coventry—*that* is the field
of the battle of so-and-so, a thousand years ago; but to get
proof of it we must search among the roots of hardy fictions
as botanists do for stifled native plants among the weeds of an
abandoned field.

The eminent French antiquarian, Louis F. A. Maury, points
out that many local dragon stories probably originated in or
have been kept alive by mistaken interpretations by the unlearned of relics, pictures, and votive offerings in churches—
the last-named including specimens of skeletons or bones of
serpents, whales and so forth, stuffed crocodiles, big fishes and
other strange animals, deposited by persons who had escaped
perils by one or another exotic beast. Formerly, at least, there
hung in the church of Mont St. Michel pieces of armour which

the peasantry held in awe as that worn by the angel Michael when he drove that old serpent, the Devil, out of heaven. At Milan, where now stands the ancient church of St. Denis, was previously a profound cavern, in which, we are told, once dwelt a dragon, always hungry, whose breath caused speedy death to any person receiving it. The Milanese hero, Viscount Uberto, killed it, according to a local legend—the basis of which is a figure, named Givre, of a heraldic dragon on the armour of an early viscount of that city. Count Aymer, of Asti, in Savoy, owes his high place in the list of dragon-slayers, says Maury, to a heraldic dragon carved at the foot of his effigy on his monumental tomb at St. Spire de Corbil. The identification of Gozon with the myth of the destruction of the dragon of Rhodes, was owing to the accidental presence near Gozon's tomb of a commonplace picture of St. George in his famous act.

How a name may serve as a punning-peg on which to hang a courtier's story or a minstrel's ballad, which later may become an element in dubious history, is shown in a *saga* of King Regnor Lodbrog, a famous pirate chief of the Viking era, who, when a young man, about the year 800, showed his mettle in an exploit of gallantry of which his companions loved to sing when the drinks went round. A Swedish prince had a beautiful daughter whom he entrusted (probably when he was sailing away on some freebooting expedition) to the care of one of his officers in a strong castle. This officer fell in love with his ward, and seizing the castle, defied the world to take her away from him. Upon this the father proclaimed abroad that whoever would conquer the ravisher and rescue the lady might have her in marriage. Of all the bold fellows who undertook the adventure Regnor alone achieved success and obtained the

191

prize. Now, it happened that the name of the faithless guardian was *Orme*, which in Icelandic means 'serpent'; wherefore the first minstrel who seized upon the incident to glorify the valour and renown of his prince (and retrieve the lady's repu-

ST. GEORGE OF THE 'GOLDEN LEGEND.'
Dutch woodcut, late fifteenth century.

tation?) represented the girl as detained in the castle by a dreadful dragon!

It is a striking fact that, although dragons and dragon-killers were commonplaces of both ancient and mediæval story-making (someone has wittily said that the dragon itself was brought into being merely as a much-needed device to exhibit the valour of more or less fictitious knights) the association of this fearsome beast with George the venerated martyr-saint, is a comparatively modern addition to his history. The oldest written account of him, that by Pasicrates, does not mention a dragon. "The Greek Church, which was naturally the first to render St. George *honour*," as Mrs. Hulst points out, "from very early times represented him with a dragon under his feet and a crowned virgin at his side, a symbolical way of saying that he overcame Sin, for the dragon represents the Devil . . . and the crowned maiden represents the Church."

This religious feeling characterized legends of such a combat found in Greek and Russian verses, and tales of a somewhat later period, but nowhere is this worshipful hero of the Church represented as fighting on horseback. The first account of a combat between St. George and a dragon that reached western Europe was in the thirteenth century in the Latin of *The Golden Legend*, where a distinctly romantic flavour tinctured the holy narrative. This epic poem became popular and spread the heroic legend, which was recited in many versions, used in dramatic representations, and led to the localizing of the adventure in many different places. Where and when this poem originated remains a mystery.

In the early part of the fifteenth century *The Golden Legend* was paraphrased by Lydgate and introduced to a few scholarly English readers in a manuscript preserved in the Bodleian Library in Oxford. It was more widely spread by Caxton, the publisher, in the translation made by him and printed in 1483. His second edition was illustrated by woodcuts borrowed from a Dutch edition of the tale, and these publications not only informed England as to the tale brought from the East, but settled the version which has been the adopted faith of our British forefathers ever since. The crabbed old English and print of Caxton's book (William Morris issued a delightful facsimile from the Kelmscott Press) are so difficult to read now that many modern renderings in both verse and prose have been produced, of which I have chosen the authentic one by Baring-Gould given below.

And so, finally, we have come to the legend of the proper, most eminent Saint George, and his most celebrated and distinguished of all Dragons—possessions peculiarly our own as Englishmen and by inheritance; and here is the creed of it for your worshipful instruction:

George, then a tribune in the Roman army, while travelling, came to Silene, a town in Libya, near which was a pond inhabited by a loathsome monster that had many times driven back an armed host sent to destroy it. It even approached the walls of the city, and with the exhalations of its breath poisoned all who came near. To prevent such visits it was given every day two sheep to satisfy its voracity. This continued until the flocks of the region were exhausted. Then the citizens held counsel and decreed that each day a man and a beast should be supplied, and at the last they had to give up their sons and daughters—none were exempted. The lot fell finally on the king's only daughter; and those who tell the story describe with vivid rhetoric the heartrending struggle of the royal father to submit to the decree, and his final victory in favour of duty to his people over his affection. So, dressed in her best, and nerved by high resolve, the princess leaves the city alone and walks toward the lake.

George, who opportunely met her on the way and saw her weeping, asked the cause of her tears. "Good youth," she exclaimed, "quickly mount your horse and fly less you perish with me." He asked her to explain the reason for so dire a prediction; and she had hardly ceased telling him when the monster lifted its head above the surface of the dark water, and the maiden, all trembling, cried again—"Fly! fly! Sir knight." His only answer was the sign of the Cross. Then he advanced to meet the horrible fiend, recommending himself to God; and brandishing his lance he transfixed the beast and cast it to the ground. Turning to the princess he bade her pass her girdle about the creature's prostrate body and to fear nothing. When this had been done the monster followed her like a docile hound. When they together had led it into the town the people fled before them, but George recalled them, bidding them put aside their fear, for the Lord had sent him to deliver them from their danger. Then the king and all his people, twenty thousand men with all their women and children, were baptized, and George smote off the head of the dragon.

Somehow, centuries ago, the people of Britain came to believe that this happened in England at Coventry; and it is no wonder that they learned and sang a *Pæan* of victory over it, comparing George's superlative bravery with the great deeds of bygone heroes. You may find it in Bishop Percy's *Reliques,* and one stanza will give you the spirit of it—

Baris conquered Ascapart, and after slew the boare,
And then he crossed the seas beyond to combat with the Moore.
Sir Isenbras and Eglamore, they were knights most bold,
And good Sir John Mandeville of travel much hath told.
There were many English knights that Pagans did convert,
But St. George, St. George, pluckt out the Dragon's heart!
   St. George he was for England; St. Dennis was for France,
     Sing: Honi soit qui mal y pense!

I have traced the dragon in time from the birth of light out of darkness to the present, and in space from the Garden of Eden eastward to farthest Cathay, and westward to the crags that withstand the Atlantic's fury. I go out where I came in: There is no dragon—there never was a dragon; but wherever in the West there *appeared* to be one there was always a St. George.

Bibliography

1. HOPKINS, E. WASHBURN. *The History of Religions.* New York, 1923.

2. WARD, WILLIAM HAYES. *Seal Cylinders of Western Asia.* New York, 1910.

3. JASTROW, MORRIS. *The Religion of Babylonia and Assyria.* Boston, 1898.

4. SMITH, G. ELLIOT. *The Evolution of the Dragon.* Manchester, 1919. Also papers in the publications of the Rylands Library in Manchester, England.

5. ST. JOHNSTON, T. R. *The Islanders of the Pacific.* London, 1921.

6. OUSELEY, SIR WILLIAM. *Travels in Persia* (Vol. II). London, 1821.

7. VISSER, M. W. DE. *The Dragon in China and Japan.* London, 1913.

8. HAVELL, E. B. *A Handbook of Indian Art.* London, 1920.

9. DEGROOT, J. J. M. *The Religious System of China.* London, 1901.

10. JOHNSTON, R. F. *Lion and Dragon in Northern China.* New York, 1910.

11. BINYON, LAURENCE. *The Flight of the Dragon.* London, 1911.

12. BUSHELL, S. W. *Chinese Art;* Handbook of the South Kensington Museum, London.

13. LAUFER, BERTHOLD. *Jade: A Study in Chinese Archæology and Religion,* Publication No. 154, Anthropological Series, Vol. X, Field Museum, Chicago, 1912. Also other of his books.

14. DINGLE, E. J. J. *Across China on Foot.* New York, 1911.

15. JOLY, HENRI L. *Legend in Japanese Art.* London, 1908.

16. BLACKER, J. F. *Chats on Oriental China.* London, 1908.

17. BALL, J. D. *Things Chinese.* London, 1900. Also other books.

18. DU BOSE, H. C. *Dragon, Image and Demon.* London, 1886.

19. GRIFFIS, WILLIAM E. *The Mikado's Empire; Corea, the Hermit Nation;* etc.

20. HAMILTON, ANGUS. *Korea.* New York, 1904.

21. HULBERT, HOMER B. *The Passing of Korea.* New York, 1906.

22. HUISH, MARCUS B. *Japan and Its Art.* London, 1913.

23. LAWSON, J. C. *Modern Greek Folklore.* Cambridge (Eng.), 1910.

24. DEANE, J. B. *Worship of the Serpent.* London, 1830.

25. CARUS, PAUL. *History of the Devil and the Idea of Evil.* Chicago, 1900.

26. CRAIGIE, W. A. *Scandinavian Folk-Lore.* London, 1896.

27. CAMPBELL, J. F. *The Celtic Dragon Myth.* Edinburgh, 1911.

28. SIKES, WIRT. *British Goblins.* London, 1880.

29. HENDERSON, W. *Folklore of the Northern Counties.* London, 1886.

*30. BULFINCH, THOMAS. *Age of Fable; Classical Myths,* etc.

31. HARTLAND, E. S. *The Legend of Perseus.* London, 1884.

32. MAURY, LOUIS F. *Essai sur les Légendes Pieuses.* Paris, 1843.

33. BARING-GOULD, SABINE. *Lives of the Saints* (Vol. IV). London, 1914.

34. CAIRD, MONA. *Romantic Cities of Provence.* London, 1906.

35. MARSHALL, H. AND H. *The Cathedral Cities of France* (Rouen). New York, 1907.

36. HULST, CORNELIA S. *St. George of Cappadocia in Legend and History.* London, 1909.

37. HOLWECK, F. G. *Dictionary of the Saints.* London, 1924.

*38. HANAUER, J. E. *Folklore of the Holy Land.* London, 1907.

*Also available as Dover reprints; for these and other related titles, log on to www.doverpublications.com

Index

201

A CATALOG OF SELECTED
DOVER BOOKS
IN ALL FIELDS OF INTEREST

A CATALOG OF SELECTED DOVER
BOOKS IN ALL FIELDS OF INTEREST

CONCERNING THE SPIRITUAL IN ART, Wassily Kandinsky. Pioneering work by father of abstract art. Thoughts on color theory, nature of art. Analysis of earlier masters. 12 illustrations. 80pp. of text. 5⅜ x 8½.   23411-8

ANIMALS: 1,419 Copyright-Free Illustrations of Mammals, Birds, Fish, Insects, etc., Jim Harter (ed.). Clear wood engravings present, in extremely lifelike poses, over 1,000 species of animals. One of the most extensive pictorial sourcebooks of its kind. Captions. Index. 284pp. 9 x 12.   23766-4

CELTIC ART: The Methods of Construction, George Bain. Simple geometric techniques for making Celtic interlacements, spirals, Kells-type initials, animals, humans, etc. Over 500 illustrations. 160pp. 9 x 12. (Available in U.S. only.)   22923-8

AN ATLAS OF ANATOMY FOR ARTISTS, Fritz Schider. Most thorough reference work on art anatomy in the world. Hundreds of illustrations, including selections from works by Vesalius, Leonardo, Goya, Ingres, Michelangelo, others. 593 illustrations. 192pp. 7⅛ x 10¼.   20241-0

CELTIC HAND STROKE-BY-STROKE (Irish Half-Uncial from "The Book of Kells"): An Arthur Baker Calligraphy Manual, Arthur Baker. Complete guide to creating each letter of the alphabet in distinctive Celtic manner. Covers hand position, strokes, pens, inks, paper, more. Illustrated. 48pp. 8¼ x 11.   24336-2

EASY ORIGAMI, John Montroll. Charming collection of 32 projects (hat, cup, pelican, piano, swan, many more) specially designed for the novice origami hobbyist. Clearly illustrated easy-to-follow instructions insure that even beginning papercrafters will achieve successful results. 48pp. 8¼ x 11.   27298-2

THE COMPLETE BOOK OF BIRDHOUSE CONSTRUCTION FOR WOOD-WORKERS, Scott D. Campbell. Detailed instructions, illustrations, tables. Also data on bird habitat and instinct patterns. Bibliography. 3 tables. 63 illustrations in 15 figures. 48pp. 5¼ x 8½.   24407-5

BLOOMINGDALE'S ILLUSTRATED 1886 CATALOG: Fashions, Dry Goods and Housewares, Bloomingdale Brothers. Famed merchants' extremely rare catalog depicting about 1,700 products: clothing, housewares, firearms, dry goods, jewelry, more. Invaluable for dating, identifying vintage items. Also, copyright-free graphics for artists, designers. Co-published with Henry Ford Museum & Greenfield Village. 160pp. 8¼ x 11.   25780-0

HISTORIC COSTUME IN PICTURES, Braun & Schneider. Over 1,450 costumed figures in clearly detailed engravings–from dawn of civilization to end of 19th century. Captions. Many folk costumes. 256pp. 8⅜ x 11¾.   23150-X

STICKLEY CRAFTSMAN FURNITURE CATALOGS, Gustav Stickley and L. & J. G. Stickley. Beautiful, functional furniture in two authentic catalogs from 1910. 594 illustrations, including 277 photos, show settles, rockers, armchairs, reclining chairs, bookcases, desks, tables. 183pp. 6½ x 9¼.   23838-5

AMERICAN LOCOMOTIVES IN HISTORIC PHOTOGRAPHS: 1858 to 1949, Ron Ziel (ed.). A rare collection of 126 meticulously detailed official photographs, called "builder portraits," of American locomotives that majestically chronicle the rise of steam locomotive power in America. Introduction. Detailed captions. xi+ 129pp. 9 x 12.   27393-8

AMERICA'S LIGHTHOUSES: An Illustrated History, Francis Ross Holland, Jr. Delightfully written, profusely illustrated fact-filled survey of over 200 American light-houses since 1716. History, anecdotes, technological advances, more. 240pp. 8 x 10¾.
25576-X

TOWARDS A NEW ARCHITECTURE, Le Corbusier. Pioneering manifesto by founder of "International School." Technical and aesthetic theories, views of industry, eco-nomics, relation of form to function, "mass-production split" and much more. Profusely illustrated. 320pp. 6⅛ x 9¼. (Available in U.S. only.)   25023-7

HOW THE OTHER HALF LIVES, Jacob Riis. Famous journalistic record, expos-ing poverty and degradation of New York slums around 1900, by major social reformer. 100 striking and influential photographs. 233pp. 10 x 7⅞.   22012-5

FRUIT KEY AND TWIG KEY TO TREES AND SHRUBS, William M. Harlow. One of the handiest and most widely used identification aids. Fruit key covers 120 deciduous and evergreen species; twig key 160 deciduous species. Easily used. Over 300 photographs. 126pp. 5⅜ x 8½.   20511-8

COMMON BIRD SONGS, Dr. Donald J. Borror. Songs of 60 most common U.S. birds: robins, sparrows, cardinals, bluejays, finches, more–arranged in order of increasing complexity. Up to 9 variations of songs of each species.
Cassette and manual 99911-4

ORCHIDS AS HOUSE PLANTS, Rebecca Tyson Northen. Grow cattleyas and many other kinds of orchids–in a window, in a case, or under artificial light. 63 illus-trations. 148pp. 5⅜ x 8½.   23261-1

MONSTER MAZES, Dave Phillips. Masterful mazes at four levels of difficulty. Avoid deadly perils and evil creatures to find magical treasures. Solutions for all 32 exciting illustrated puzzles. 48pp. 8¼ x 11.   26005-4

MOZART'S DON GIOVANNI (DOVER OPERA LIBRETTO SERIES), Wolfgang Amadeus Mozart. Introduced and translated by Ellen H. Bleiler. Standard Italian libretto, with complete English translation. Convenient and thoroughly portable–an ideal companion for reading along with a recording or the performance itself. Introduction. List of characters. Plot summary. 121pp. 5¼ x 8½.   24944-1

TECHNICAL MANUAL AND DICTIONARY OF CLASSICAL BALLET, Gail Grant. Defines, explains, comments on steps, movements, poses and concepts. 15-page pictorial section. Basic book for student, viewer. 127pp. 5⅜ x 8½.   21843-0

THE CLARINET AND CLARINET PLAYING, David Pino. Lively, comprehensive work features suggestions about technique, musicianship, and musical interpretation, as well as guidelines for teaching, making your own reeds, and preparing for public performance. Includes an intriguing look at clarinet history. "A godsend," *The Clarinet,* Journal of the International Clarinet Society. Appendixes. 7 illus. 320pp. 5⅜ x 8½. 40270-3

HOLLYWOOD GLAMOR PORTRAITS, John Kobal (ed.). 145 photos from 1926-49. Harlow, Gable, Bogart, Bacall; 94 stars in all. Full background on photographers, technical aspects. 160pp. 8⅜ x 11¼. 23352-9

THE ANNOTATED CASEY AT THE BAT: A Collection of Ballads about the Mighty Casey/Third, Revised Edition, Martin Gardner (ed.). Amusing sequels and parodies of one of America's best-loved poems: Casey's Revenge, Why Casey Whiffed, Casey's Sister at the Bat, others. 256pp. 5⅜ x 8½. 28598-7

THE RAVEN AND OTHER FAVORITE POEMS, Edgar Allan Poe. Over 40 of the author's most memorable poems: "The Bells," "Ulalume," "Israfel," "To Helen," "The Conqueror Worm," "Eldorado," "Annabel Lee," many more. Alphabetic lists of titles and first lines. 64pp. 5³⁄₁₆ x 8¼. 26685-0

PERSONAL MEMOIRS OF U. S. GRANT, Ulysses Simpson Grant. Intelligent, deeply moving firsthand account of Civil War campaigns, considered by many the finest military memoirs ever written. Includes letters, historic photographs, maps and more. 528pp. 6⅛ x 9¼. 28587-1

ANCIENT EGYPTIAN MATERIALS AND INDUSTRIES, A. Lucas and J. Harris. Fascinating, comprehensive, thoroughly documented text describes this ancient civilization's vast resources and the processes that incorporated them in daily life, including the use of animal products, building materials, cosmetics, perfumes and incense, fibers, glazed ware, glass and its manufacture, materials used in the mummification process, and much more. 544pp. 6⅛ x 9¼. (Available in U.S. only.) 40446-3

RUSSIAN STORIES/RUSSKIE RASSKAZY: A Dual-Language Book, edited by Gleb Struve. Twelve tales by such masters as Chekhov, Tolstoy, Dostoevsky, Pushkin, others. Excellent word-for-word English translations on facing pages, plus teaching and study aids, Russian/English vocabulary, biographical/critical introductions, more. 416pp. 5⅜ x 8½. 26244-8

PHILADELPHIA THEN AND NOW: 60 Sites Photographed in the Past and Present, Kenneth Finkel and Susan Oyama. Rare photographs of City Hall, Logan Square, Independence Hall, Betsy Ross House, other landmarks juxtaposed with contemporary views. Captures changing face of historic city. Introduction. Captions. 128pp. 8¼ x 11. 25790-8

AIA ARCHITECTURAL GUIDE TO NASSAU AND SUFFOLK COUNTIES, LONG ISLAND, The American Institute of Architects, Long Island Chapter, and the Society for the Preservation of Long Island Antiquities. Comprehensive, well-researched and generously illustrated volume brings to life over three centuries of Long Island's great architectural heritage. More than 240 photographs with authoritative, extensively detailed captions. 176pp. 8¼ x 11. 26946-9

NORTH AMERICAN INDIAN LIFE: Customs and Traditions of 23 Tribes, Elsie Clews Parsons (ed.). 27 fictionalized essays by noted anthropologists examine religion, customs, government, additional facets of life among the Winnebago, Crow, Zuni, Eskimo, other tribes. 480pp. 6⅛ x 9¼. 27377-6

FRANK LLOYD WRIGHT'S DANA HOUSE, Donald Hoffmann. Pictorial essay of residential masterpiece with over 160 interior and exterior photos, plans, elevations, sketches and studies. 128pp. 9¼ x 10¾. 29120-0

THE MALE AND FEMALE FIGURE IN MOTION: 60 Classic Photographic Sequences, Eadweard Muybridge. 60 true-action photographs of men and women walking, running, climbing, bending, turning, etc., reproduced from rare 19th-century masterpiece. vi + 121pp. 9 x 12. 24745-7

1001 QUESTIONS ANSWERED ABOUT THE SEASHORE, N. J. Berrill and Jacquelyn Berrill. Queries answered about dolphins, sea snails, sponges, starfish, fishes, shore birds, many others. Covers appearance, breeding, growth, feeding, much more. 305pp. 5¼ x 8¼. 23366-9

ATTRACTING BIRDS TO YOUR YARD, William J. Weber. Easy-to-follow guide offers advice on how to attract the greatest diversity of birds: birdhouses, feeders, water and waterers, much more. 96pp. 5³⁄₁₆ x 8¼. 28927-3

MEDICINAL AND OTHER USES OF NORTH AMERICAN PLANTS: A Historical Survey with Special Reference to the Eastern Indian Tribes, Charlotte Erichsen-Brown. Chronological historical citations document 500 years of usage of plants, trees, shrubs native to eastern Canada, northeastern U.S. Also complete identifying information. 343 illustrations. 544pp. 6½ x 9¼. 25951-X

STORYBOOK MAZES, Dave Phillips. 23 stories and mazes on two-page spreads: Wizard of Oz, Treasure Island, Robin Hood, etc. Solutions. 64pp. 8¼ x 11. 23628-5

AMERICAN NEGRO SONGS: 230 Folk Songs and Spirituals, Religious and Secular, John W. Work. This authoritative study traces the African influences of songs sung and played by black Americans at work, in church, and as entertainment. The author discusses the lyric significance of such songs as "Swing Low, Sweet Chariot," "John Henry," and others and offers the words and music for 230 songs. Bibliography. Index of Song Titles. 272pp. 6½ x 9¼. 40271-1

MOVIE-STAR PORTRAITS OF THE FORTIES, John Kobal (ed.). 163 glamor, studio photos of 106 stars of the 1940s: Rita Hayworth, Ava Gardner, Marlon Brando, Clark Gable, many more. 176pp. 8⅜ x 11¼. 23546-7

BENCHLEY LOST AND FOUND, Robert Benchley. Finest humor from early 30s, about pet peeves, child psychologists, post office and others. Mostly unavailable elsewhere. 73 illustrations by Peter Arno and others. 183pp. 5⅜ x 8½. 22410-4

YEKL and THE IMPORTED BRIDEGROOM AND OTHER STORIES OF YIDDISH NEW YORK, Abraham Cahan. Film Hester Street based on *Yekl* (1896). Novel, other stories among first about Jewish immigrants on N.Y.'s East Side. 240pp. 5⅜ x 8½. 22427-9

SELECTED POEMS, Walt Whitman. Generous sampling from *Leaves of Grass*. Twenty-four poems include "I Hear America Singing," "Song of the Open Road," "I Sing the Body Electric," "When Lilacs Last in the Dooryard Bloom'd," "O Captain! My Captain!"–all reprinted from an authoritative edition. Lists of titles and first lines. 128pp. 5³⁄₁₆ x 8¼. 26878-0

THE BEST TALES OF HOFFMANN, E. T. A. Hoffmann. 10 of Hoffmann's most important stories: "Nutcracker and the King of Mice," "The Golden Flowerpot," etc. 458pp. 5⅜ x 8½. 21793-0

FROM FETISH TO GOD IN ANCIENT EGYPT, E. A. Wallis Budge. Rich detailed survey of Egyptian conception of "God" and gods, magic, cult of animals, Osiris, more. Also, superb English translations of hymns and legends. 240 illustrations. 545pp. 5⅜ x 8½. 25803-3

FRENCH STORIES/CONTES FRANÇAIS: A Dual-Language Book, Wallace Fowlie. Ten stories by French masters, Voltaire to Camus: "Micromegas" by Voltaire; "The Atheist's Mass" by Balzac; "Minuet" by de Maupassant; "The Guest" by Camus, six more. Excellent English translations on facing pages. Also French-English vocabulary list, exercises, more. 352pp. 5⅜ x 8½. 26443-2

CHICAGO AT THE TURN OF THE CENTURY IN PHOTOGRAPHS: 122 Historic Views from the Collections of the Chicago Historical Society, Larry A. Viskochil. Rare large-format prints offer detailed views of City Hall, State Street, the Loop, Hull House, Union Station, many other landmarks, circa 1904-1913. Introduction. Captions. Maps. 144pp. 9⅜ x 12¼. 24656-6

OLD BROOKLYN IN EARLY PHOTOGRAPHS, 1865-1929, William Lee Younger. Luna Park, Gravesend race track, construction of Grand Army Plaza, moving of Hotel Brighton, etc. 157 previously unpublished photographs. 165pp. 8⅞ x 11¾. 23587-4

THE MYTHS OF THE NORTH AMERICAN INDIANS, Lewis Spence. Rich anthology of the myths and legends of the Algonquins, Iroquois, Pawnees and Sioux, prefaced by an extensive historical and ethnological commentary. 36 illustrations. 480pp. 5⅜ x 8½. 25967-6

AN ENCYCLOPEDIA OF BATTLES: Accounts of Over 1,560 Battles from 1479 B.C. to the Present, David Eggenberger. Essential details of every major battle in recorded history from the first battle of Megiddo in 1479 B.C. to Grenada in 1984. List of Battle Maps. New Appendix covering the years 1967-1984. Index. 99 illustrations. 544pp. 6½ x 9¼. 24913-1

SAILING ALONE AROUND THE WORLD, Captain Joshua Slocum. First man to sail around the world, alone, in small boat. One of great feats of seamanship told in delightful manner. 67 illustrations. 294pp. 5⅜ x 8½. 20326-3

ANARCHISM AND OTHER ESSAYS, Emma Goldman. Powerful, penetrating, prophetic essays on direct action, role of minorities, prison reform, puritan hypocrisy, violence, etc. 271pp. 5⅜ x 8½. 22484-8

MYTHS OF THE HINDUS AND BUDDHISTS, Ananda K. Coomaraswamy and Sister Nivedita. Great stories of the epics; deeds of Krishna, Shiva, taken from puranas, Vedas, folk tales; etc. 32 illustrations. 400pp. 5⅜ x 8½. 21759-0

THE TRAUMA OF BIRTH, Otto Rank. Rank's controversial thesis that anxiety neurosis is caused by profound psychological trauma which occurs at birth. 256pp. 5⅜ x 8½. 27974-X

A THEOLOGICO-POLITICAL TREATISE, Benedict Spinoza. Also contains unfinished Political Treatise. Great classic on religious liberty, theory of government on common consent. R. Elwes translation. Total of 421pp. 5⅜ x 8½. 20249-6

MY BONDAGE AND MY FREEDOM, Frederick Douglass. Born a slave, Douglass became outspoken force in antislavery movement. The best of Douglass' autobiographies. Graphic description of slave life. 464pp. 5⅜ x 8½. 22457-0

FOLLOWING THE EQUATOR: A Journey Around the World, Mark Twain. Fascinating humorous account of 1897 voyage to Hawaii, Australia, India, New Zealand, etc. Ironic, bemused reports on peoples, customs, climate, flora and fauna, politics, much more. 197 illustrations. 720pp. 5⅜ x 8½. 26113-1

THE PEOPLE CALLED SHAKERS, Edward D. Andrews. Definitive study of Shakers: origins, beliefs, practices, dances, social organization, furniture and crafts, etc. 33 illustrations. 351pp. 5⅜ x 8½. 21081-2

THE MYTHS OF GREECE AND ROME, H. A. Guerber. A classic of mythology, generously illustrated, long prized for its simple, graphic, accurate retelling of the principal myths of Greece and Rome, and for its commentary on their origins and significance. With 64 illustrations by Michelangelo, Raphael, Titian, Rubens, Canova, Bernini and others. 480pp. 5⅜ x 8½. 27584-1

PSYCHOLOGY OF MUSIC, Carl E. Seashore. Classic work discusses music as a medium from psychological viewpoint. Clear treatment of physical acoustics, auditory apparatus, sound perception, development of musical skills, nature of musical feeling, host of other topics. 88 figures. 408pp. 5⅜ x 8½. 21851-1

THE PHILOSOPHY OF HISTORY, Georg W. Hegel. Great classic of Western thought develops concept that history is not chance but rational process, the evolution of freedom. 457pp. 5⅜ x 8½. 20112-0

THE BOOK OF TEA, Kakuzo Okakura. Minor classic of the Orient: entertaining, charming explanation, interpretation of traditional Japanese culture in terms of tea ceremony. 94pp. 5⅜ x 8½. 20070-1

LIFE IN ANCIENT EGYPT, Adolf Erman. Fullest, most thorough, detailed older account with much not in more recent books, domestic life, religion, magic, medicine, commerce, much more. Many illustrations reproduce tomb paintings, carvings, hieroglyphs, etc. 597pp. 5⅜ x 8½. 22632-8

SUNDIALS, Their Theory and Construction, Albert Waugh. Far and away the best, most thorough coverage of ideas, mathematics concerned, types, construction, adjusting anywhere. Simple, nontechnical treatment allows even children to build several of these dials. Over 100 illustrations. 230pp. 5⅜ x 8½. 22947-5

THEORETICAL HYDRODYNAMICS, L. M. Milne-Thomson. Classic exposition of the mathematical theory of fluid motion, applicable to both hydrodynamics and aerodynamics. Over 600 exercises. 768pp. 6⅛ x 9¼. 68970-0

SONGS OF EXPERIENCE: Facsimile Reproduction with 26 Plates in Full Color, William Blake. 26 full-color plates from a rare 1826 edition. Includes "The Tyger," "London," "Holy Thursday," and other poems. Printed text of poems. 48pp. 5¼ x 7. 24636-1

OLD-TIME VIGNETTES IN FULL COLOR, Carol Belanger Grafton (ed.). Over 390 charming, often sentimental illustrations, selected from archives of Victorian graphics—pretty women posing, children playing, food, flowers, kittens and puppies, smiling cherubs, birds and butterflies, much more. All copyright-free. 48pp. 9¼ x 12¼. 27269-9

PERSPECTIVE FOR ARTISTS, Rex Vicat Cole. Depth, perspective of sky and sea, shadows, much more, not usually covered. 391 diagrams, 81 reproductions of drawings and paintings. 279pp. 5⅜ x 8½. 22487-2

DRAWING THE LIVING FIGURE, Joseph Sheppard. Innovative approach to artistic anatomy focuses on specifics of surface anatomy, rather than muscles and bones. Over 170 drawings of live models in front, back and side views, and in widely varying poses. Accompanying diagrams. 177 illustrations. Introduction. Index. 144pp. 8⅜ x11¼. 26723-7

GOTHIC AND OLD ENGLISH ALPHABETS: 100 Complete Fonts, Dan X. Solo. Add power, elegance to posters, signs, other graphics with 100 stunning copyright-free alphabets: Blackstone, Dolbey, Germania, 97 more—including many lower-case, numerals, punctuation marks. 104pp. 8⅛ x 11. 24695-7

HOW TO DO BEADWORK, Mary White. Fundamental book on craft from simple projects to five-bead chains and woven works. 106 illustrations. 142pp. 5⅜ x 8.

20697-1

THE BOOK OF WOOD CARVING, Charles Marshall Sayers. Finest book for beginners discusses fundamentals and offers 34 designs. "Absolutely first rate . . . well thought out and well executed."—E. J. Tangerman. 118pp. 7¾ x 10⅝. 23654-4

ILLUSTRATED CATALOG OF CIVIL WAR MILITARY GOODS: Union Army Weapons, Insignia, Uniform Accessories, and Other Equipment, Schuyler, Hartley, and Graham. Rare, profusely illustrated 1846 catalog includes Union Army uniform and dress regulations, arms and ammunition, coats, insignia, flags, swords, rifles, etc. 226 illustrations. 160pp. 9 x 12. 24939-5

WOMEN'S FASHIONS OF THE EARLY 1900s: An Unabridged Republication of "New York Fashions, 1909," National Cloak & Suit Co. Rare catalog of mail-order fashions documents women's and children's clothing styles shortly after the turn of the century. Captions offer full descriptions, prices. Invaluable resource for fashion, costume historians. Approximately 725 illustrations. 128pp. 8⅜ x 11¼. 27276-1

THE 1912 AND 1915 GUSTAV STICKLEY FURNITURE CATALOGS, Gustav Stickley. With over 200 detailed illustrations and descriptions, these two catalogs are essential reading and reference materials and identification guides for Stickley furniture. Captions cite materials, dimensions and prices. 112pp. 6½ x 9¼. 26676-1

EARLY AMERICAN LOCOMOTIVES, John H. White, Jr. Finest locomotive engravings from early 19th century: historical (1804–74), main-line (after 1870), special, foreign, etc. 147 plates. 142pp. 11⅜ x 8¼. 22772-3

THE TALL SHIPS OF TODAY IN PHOTOGRAPHS, Frank O. Braynard. Lavishly illustrated tribute to nearly 100 majestic contemporary sailing vessels: Amerigo Vespucci, Clearwater, Constitution, Eagle, Mayflower, Sea Cloud, Victory, many more. Authoritative captions provide statistics, background on each ship. 190 black-and-white photographs and illustrations. Introduction. 128pp. 8⅞ x 11¾.

27163-3

LITTLE BOOK OF EARLY AMERICAN CRAFTS AND TRADES, Peter Stockham (ed.). 1807 children's book explains crafts and trades: baker, hatter, cooper, potter, and many others. 23 copperplate illustrations. 140pp. 4⅝ x 6. 23336-7

VICTORIAN FASHIONS AND COSTUMES FROM HARPER'S BAZAR, 1867–1898, Stella Blum (ed.). Day costumes, evening wear, sports clothes, shoes, hats, other accessories in over 1,000 detailed engravings. 320pp. 9⅜ x 12¼. 22990-4

GUSTAV STICKLEY, THE CRAFTSMAN, Mary Ann Smith. Superb study surveys broad scope of Stickley's achievement, especially in architecture. Design philosophy, rise and fall of the Craftsman empire, descriptions and floor plans for many Craftsman houses, more. 86 black-and-white halftones. 31 line illustrations. Introduction 208pp. 6½ x 9¼. 27210-9

THE LONG ISLAND RAIL ROAD IN EARLY PHOTOGRAPHS, Ron Ziel. Over 220 rare photos, informative text document origin (1844) and development of rail service on Long Island. Vintage views of early trains, locomotives, stations, passengers, crews, much more. Captions. 8⅞ x 11¾. 26301-0

VOYAGE OF THE LIBERDADE, Joshua Slocum. Great 19th-century mariner's thrilling, first-hand account of the wreck of his ship off South America, the 35-foot boat he built from the wreckage, and its remarkable voyage home. 128pp. 5⅜ x 8½. 40022-0

TEN BOOKS ON ARCHITECTURE, Vitruvius. The most important book ever written on architecture. Early Roman aesthetics, technology, classical orders, site selection, all other aspects. Morgan translation. 331pp. 5⅜ x 8½. 20645-9

THE HUMAN FIGURE IN MOTION, Eadweard Muybridge. More than 4,500 stopped-action photos, in action series, showing undraped men, women, children jumping, lying down, throwing, sitting, wrestling, carrying, etc. 390pp. 7⅞ x 10⅝. 20204-6 Clothbd.

TREES OF THE EASTERN AND CENTRAL UNITED STATES AND CANADA, William M. Harlow. Best one-volume guide to 140 trees. Full descriptions, woodlore, range, etc. Over 600 illustrations. Handy size. 288pp. 4½ x 6⅜. 20395-6

SONGS OF WESTERN BIRDS, Dr. Donald J. Borror. Complete song and call repertoire of 60 western species, including flycatchers, juncoes, cactus wrens, many more—includes fully illustrated booklet. Cassette and manual 99913-0

GROWING AND USING HERBS AND SPICES, Milo Miloradovich. Versatile handbook provides all the information needed for cultivation and use of all the herbs and spices available in North America. 4 illustrations. Index. Glossary. 236pp. 5⅜ x 8½. 25058-X

BIG BOOK OF MAZES AND LABYRINTHS, Walter Shepherd. 50 mazes and labyrinths in all—classical, solid, ripple, and more—in one great volume. Perfect inexpensive puzzler for clever youngsters. Full solutions. 112pp. 8⅛ x 11. 22951-3

PIANO TUNING, J. Cree Fischer. Clearest, best book for beginner, amateur. Simple repairs, raising dropped notes, tuning by easy method of flattened fifths. No previous skills needed. 4 illustrations. 201pp. 5⅜ x 8½. 23267-0

HINTS TO SINGERS, Lillian Nordica. Selecting the right teacher, developing confidence, overcoming stage fright, and many other important skills receive thoughtful discussion in this indispensible guide, written by a world-famous diva of four decades' experience. 96pp. 5⅜ x 8½. 40094-8

THE COMPLETE NONSENSE OF EDWARD LEAR, Edward Lear. All nonsense limericks, zany alphabets, Owl and Pussycat, songs, nonsense botany, etc., illustrated by Lear. Total of 320pp. 5⅜ x 8½. (Available in U.S. only.) 20167-8

VICTORIAN PARLOUR POETRY: An Annotated Anthology, Michael R. Turner. 117 gems by Longfellow, Tennyson, Browning, many lesser-known poets. "The Village Blacksmith," "Curfew Must Not Ring Tonight," "Only a Baby Small," dozens more, often difficult to find elsewhere. Index of poets, titles, first lines. xxiii + 325pp. 5⅝ x 8¼. 27044-0

DUBLINERS, James Joyce. Fifteen stories offer vivid, tightly focused observations of the lives of Dublin's poorer classes. At least one, "The Dead," is considered a masterpiece. Reprinted complete and unabridged from standard edition. 160pp. 5$^{3}/_{16}$ x 8¼. 26870-5

GREAT WEIRD TALES: 14 Stories by Lovecraft, Blackwood, Machen and Others, S. T. Joshi (ed.). 14 spellbinding tales, including "The Sin Eater," by Fiona McLeod, "The Eye Above the Mantel," by Frank Belknap Long, as well as renowned works by R. H. Barlow, Lord Dunsany, Arthur Machen, W. C. Morrow and eight other masters of the genre. 256pp. 5⅜ x 8½. (Available in U.S. only.) 40436-6

THE BOOK OF THE SACRED MAGIC OF ABRAMELIN THE MAGE, translated by S. MacGregor Mathers. Medieval manuscript of ceremonial magic. Basic document in Aleister Crowley, Golden Dawn groups. 268pp. 5⅜ x 8½. 23211-5

NEW RUSSIAN-ENGLISH AND ENGLISH-RUSSIAN DICTIONARY, M. A. O'Brien. This is a remarkably handy Russian dictionary, containing a surprising amount of information, including over 70,000 entries. 366pp. 4½ x 6⅛. 20208-9

HISTORIC HOMES OF THE AMERICAN PRESIDENTS, Second, Revised Edition, Irvin Haas. A traveler's guide to American Presidential homes, most open to the public, depicting and describing homes occupied by every American President from George Washington to George Bush. With visiting hours, admission charges, travel routes. 175 photographs. Index. 160pp. 8¼ x 11. 26751-2

NEW YORK IN THE FORTIES, Andreas Feininger. 162 brilliant photographs by the well-known photographer, formerly with *Life* magazine. Commuters, shoppers, Times Square at night, much else from city at its peak. Captions by John von Hartz. 181pp. 9¼ x 10¾. 23585-8

INDIAN SIGN LANGUAGE, William Tomkins. Over 525 signs developed by Sioux and other tribes. Written instructions and diagrams. Also 290 pictographs. 111pp. 6⅛ x 9¼. 22029-X

CATALOG OF DOVER BOOKS

ANATOMY: A Complete Guide for Artists, Joseph Sheppard. A master of figure drawing shows artists how to render human anatomy convincingly. Over 460 illustrations. 224pp. 8⅜ x 11¼. 27279-6

MEDIEVAL CALLIGRAPHY: Its History and Technique, Marc Drogin. Spirited history, comprehensive instruction manual covers 13 styles (ca. 4th century through 15th). Excellent photographs; directions for duplicating medieval techniques with modern tools. 224pp. 8⅜ x 11¼. 26142-5

DRIED FLOWERS: How to Prepare Them, Sarah Whitlock and Martha Rankin. Complete instructions on how to use silica gel, meal and borax, perlite aggregate, sand and borax, glycerine and water to create attractive permanent flower arrangements. 12 illustrations. 32pp. 5⅜ x 8½. 21802-3

EASY-TO-MAKE BIRD FEEDERS FOR WOODWORKERS, Scott D. Campbell. Detailed, simple-to-use guide for designing, constructing, caring for and using feeders. Text, illustrations for 12 classic and contemporary designs. 96pp. 5⅜ x 8½. 25847-5

SCOTTISH WONDER TALES FROM MYTH AND LEGEND, Donald A. Mackenzie. 16 lively tales tell of giants rumbling down mountainsides, of a magic wand that turns stone pillars into warriors, of gods and goddesses, evil hags, powerful forces and more. 240pp. 5⅜ x 8½. 29677-6

THE HISTORY OF UNDERCLOTHES, C. Willett Cunnington and Phyllis Cunnington. Fascinating, well-documented survey covering six centuries of English undergarments, enhanced with over 100 illustrations: 12th-century laced-up bodice, footed long drawers (1795), 19th-century bustles, 19th-century corsets for men, Victorian "bust improvers," much more. 272pp. 5⅝ x 8¼. 27124-2

ARTS AND CRAFTS FURNITURE: The Complete Brooks Catalog of 1912, Brooks Manufacturing Co. Photos and detailed descriptions of more than 150 now very collectible furniture designs from the Arts and Crafts movement depict davenports, settees, buffets, desks, tables, chairs, bedsteads, dressers and more, all built of solid, quarter-sawed oak. Invaluable for students and enthusiasts of antiques, Americana and the decorative arts. 80pp. 6½ x 9¼. 27471-3

WILBUR AND ORVILLE: A Biography of the Wright Brothers, Fred Howard. Definitive, crisply written study tells the full story of the brothers' lives and work. A vividly written biography, unparalleled in scope and color, that also captures the spirit of an extraordinary era. 560pp. 6⅛ x 9¼. 40297-5

THE ARTS OF THE SAILOR: Knotting, Splicing and Ropework, Hervey Garrett Smith. Indispensable shipboard reference covers tools, basic knots and useful hitches; handsewing and canvas work, more. Over 100 illustrations. Delightful reading for sea lovers. 256pp. 5⅜ x 8½. 26440-8

FRANK LLOYD WRIGHT'S FALLINGWATER: The House and Its History, Second, Revised Edition, Donald Hoffmann. A total revision–both in text and illustrations–of the standard document on Fallingwater, the boldest, most personal architectural statement of Wright's mature years, updated with valuable new material from the recently opened Frank Lloyd Wright Archives. "Fascinating"–*The New York Times.* 116 illustrations. 128pp. 9¼ x 10¾. 27430-6

PHOTOGRAPHIC SKETCHBOOK OF THE CIVIL WAR, Alexander Gardner. 100 photos taken on field during the Civil War. Famous shots of Manassas Harper's Ferry, Lincoln, Richmond, slave pens, etc. 244pp. 10⅝ x 8¼. 22731-6

FIVE ACRES AND INDEPENDENCE, Maurice G. Kains. Great back-to-the-land classic explains basics of self-sufficient farming. The one book to get. 95 illustrations. 397pp. 5⅜ x 8½. 20974-1

SONGS OF EASTERN BIRDS, Dr. Donald J. Borror. Songs and calls of 60 species most common to eastern U.S.: warblers, woodpeckers, flycatchers, thrushes, larks, many more in high-quality recording. Cassette and manual 99912-2

A MODERN HERBAL, Margaret Grieve. Much the fullest, most exact, most useful compilation of herbal material. Gigantic alphabetical encyclopedia, from aconite to zedoary, gives botanical information, medical properties, folklore, economic uses, much else. Indispensable to serious reader. 161 illustrations. 888pp. 6½ x 9¼. 2-vol. set. (Available in U.S. only.) Vol. I: 22798-7
Vol. II: 22799-5

HIDDEN TREASURE MAZE BOOK, Dave Phillips. Solve 34 challenging mazes accompanied by heroic tales of adventure. Evil dragons, people-eating plants, blood-thirsty giants, many more dangerous adversaries lurk at every twist and turn. 34 mazes, stories, solutions. 48pp. 8¼ x 11. 24566-7

LETTERS OF W. A. MOZART, Wolfgang A. Mozart. Remarkable letters show bawdy wit, humor, imagination, musical insights, contemporary musical world; includes some letters from Leopold Mozart. 276pp. 5⅜ x 8½. 22859-2

BASIC PRINCIPLES OF CLASSICAL BALLET, Agrippina Vaganova. Great Russian theoretician, teacher explains methods for teaching classical ballet. 118 illustrations. 175pp. 5⅜ x 8½. 22036-2

THE JUMPING FROG, Mark Twain. Revenge edition. The original story of The Celebrated Jumping Frog of Calaveras County, a hapless French translation, and Twain's hilarious "retranslation" from the French. 12 illustrations. 66pp. 5⅜ x 8½. 22686-7

BEST REMEMBERED POEMS, Martin Gardner (ed.). The 126 poems in this superb collection of 19th- and 20th-century British and American verse range from Shelley's "To a Skylark" to the impassioned "Renascence" of Edna St. Vincent Millay and to Edward Lear's whimsical "The Owl and the Pussycat." 224pp. 5⅜ x 8½. 27165-X

COMPLETE SONNETS, William Shakespeare. Over 150 exquisite poems deal with love, friendship, the tyranny of time, beauty's evanescence, death and other themes in language of remarkable power, precision and beauty. Glossary of archaic terms. 80pp. 5³⁄₁₆ x 8¼. 26686-9

THE BATTLES THAT CHANGED HISTORY, Fletcher Pratt. Eminent historian profiles 16 crucial conflicts, ancient to modern, that changed the course of civilization. 352pp. 5⅜ x 8½. 41129-X

THE WIT AND HUMOR OF OSCAR WILDE, Alvin Redman (ed.). More than 1,000 ripostes, paradoxes, wisecracks: Work is the curse of the drinking classes; I can resist everything except temptation; etc. 258pp. 5⅜ x 8½. 20602-5

SHAKESPEARE LEXICON AND QUOTATION DICTIONARY, Alexander Schmidt. Full definitions, locations, shades of meaning in every word in plays and poems. More than 50,000 exact quotations. 1,485pp. 6½ x 9¼. 2-vol. set.
Vol. 1: 22726-X
Vol. 2: 22727-8

SELECTED POEMS, Emily Dickinson. Over 100 best-known, best-loved poems by one of America's foremost poets, reprinted from authoritative early editions. No comparable edition at this price. Index of first lines. 64pp. 5$\frac{3}{16}$ x 8¼. 26466-1

THE INSIDIOUS DR. FU-MANCHU, Sax Rohmer. The first of the popular mystery series introduces a pair of English detectives to their archnemesis, the diabolical Dr. Fu-Manchu. Flavorful atmosphere, fast-paced action, and colorful characters enliven this classic of the genre. 208pp. 5$\frac{3}{16}$ x 8¼. 29898-1

THE MALLEUS MALEFICARUM OF KRAMER AND SPRENGER, translated by Montague Summers. Full text of most important witchhunter's "bible," used by both Catholics and Protestants. 278pp. 6⅝ x 10. 22802-9

SPANISH STORIES/CUENTOS ESPAÑOLES: A Dual-Language Book, Angel Flores (ed.). Unique format offers 13 great stories in Spanish by Cervantes, Borges, others. Faithful English translations on facing pages. 352pp. 5⅜ x 8½. 25399-6

GARDEN CITY, LONG ISLAND, IN EARLY PHOTOGRAPHS, 1869–1919, Mildred H. Smith. Handsome treasury of 118 vintage pictures, accompanied by carefully researched captions, document the Garden City Hotel fire (1899), the Vanderbilt Cup Race (1908), the first airmail flight departing from the Nassau Boulevard Aerodrome (1911), and much more. 96pp. 8⅞ x 11¾. 40669-5

OLD QUEENS, N.Y., IN EARLY PHOTOGRAPHS, Vincent F. Seyfried and William Asadorian. Over 160 rare photographs of Maspeth, Jamaica, Jackson Heights, and other areas. Vintage views of DeWitt Clinton mansion, 1939 World's Fair and more. Captions. 192pp. 8⅞ x 11. 26358-4

CAPTURED BY THE INDIANS: 15 Firsthand Accounts, 1750-1870, Frederick Drimmer. Astounding true historical accounts of grisly torture, bloody conflicts, relentless pursuits, miraculous escapes and more, by people who lived to tell the tale. 384pp. 5⅜ x 8½. 24901-8

THE WORLD'S GREAT SPEECHES (Fourth Enlarged Edition), Lewis Copeland, Lawrence W. Lamm, and Stephen J. McKenna. Nearly 300 speeches provide public speakers with a wealth of updated quotes and inspiration–from Pericles' funeral oration and William Jennings Bryan's "Cross of Gold Speech" to Malcolm X's powerful words on the Black Revolution and Earl of Spenser's tribute to his sister, Diana, Princess of Wales. 944pp. 5⅜ x 8⅜. 40903-1

THE BOOK OF THE SWORD, Sir Richard F. Burton. Great Victorian scholar/adventurer's eloquent, erudite history of the "queen of weapons"–from prehistory to early Roman Empire. Evolution and development of early swords, variations (sabre, broadsword, cutlass, scimitar, etc.), much more. 336pp. 6⅛ x 9¼.
25434-8

AUTOBIOGRAPHY: The Story of My Experiments with Truth, Mohandas K. Gandhi. Boyhood, legal studies, purification, the growth of the Satyagraha (nonviolent protest) movement. Critical, inspiring work of the man responsible for the freedom of India. 480pp. 5⅜ x 8½. (Available in U.S. only.) 24593-4

CELTIC MYTHS AND LEGENDS, T. W. Rolleston. Masterful retelling of Irish and Welsh stories and tales. Cuchulain, King Arthur, Deirdre, the Grail, many more. First paperback edition. 58 full-page illustrations. 512pp. 5⅜ x 8½. 26507-2

THE PRINCIPLES OF PSYCHOLOGY, William James. Famous long course complete, unabridged. Stream of thought, time perception, memory, experimental methods; great work decades ahead of its time. 94 figures. 1,391pp. 5⅜ x 8½. 2-vol. set.
Vol. I: 20381-6   Vol. II: 20382-4

THE WORLD AS WILL AND REPRESENTATION, Arthur Schopenhauer. Definitive English translation of Schopenhauer's life work, correcting more than 1,000 errors, omissions in earlier translations. Translated by E. F. J. Payne. Total of 1,269pp. 5⅜ x 8½. 2-vol. set.
Vol. 1: 21761-2   Vol. 2: 21762-0

MAGIC AND MYSTERY IN TIBET, Madame Alexandra David-Neel. Experiences among lamas, magicians, sages, sorcerers, Bonpa wizards. A true psychic discovery. 32 illustrations. 321pp. 5⅜ x 8½. (Available in U.S. only.) 22682-4

THE EGYPTIAN BOOK OF THE DEAD, E. A. Wallis Budge. Complete reproduction of Ani's papyrus, finest ever found. Full hieroglyphic text, interlinear transliteration, word-for-word translation, smooth translation. 533pp. 6½ x 9¼. 21866-X

MATHEMATICS FOR THE NONMATHEMATICIAN, Morris Kline. Detailed, college-level treatment of mathematics in cultural and historical context, with numerous exercises. Recommended Reading Lists. Tables. Numerous figures. 641pp. 5⅜ x 8½. 24823-2

PROBABILISTIC METHODS IN THE THEORY OF STRUCTURES, Isaac Elishakoff. Well-written introduction covers the elements of the theory of probability from two or more random variables, the reliability of such multivariable structures, the theory of random function, Monte Carlo methods of treating problems incapable of exact solution, and more. Examples. 502pp. 5⅜ x 8½. 40691-1

THE RIME OF THE ANCIENT MARINER, Gustave Doré, S. T. Coleridge. Doré's finest work; 34 plates capture moods, subtleties of poem. Flawless full-size reproductions printed on facing pages with authoritative text of poem. "Beautiful. Simply beautiful."–*Publisher's Weekly.* 77pp. 9¼ x 12. 22305-1

NORTH AMERICAN INDIAN DESIGNS FOR ARTISTS AND CRAFTSPEOPLE, Eva Wilson. Over 360 authentic copyright-free designs adapted from Navajo blankets, Hopi pottery, Sioux buffalo hides, more. Geometrics, symbolic figures, plant and animal motifs, etc. 128pp. 8⅜ x 11. (Not for sale in the United Kingdom.) 25341-4

SCULPTURE: Principles and Practice, Louis Slobodkin. Step-by-step approach to clay, plaster, metals, stone; classical and modern. 253 drawings, photos. 255pp. 8⅛ x 11. 22960-2

THE INFLUENCE OF SEA POWER UPON HISTORY, 1660–1783, A. T. Mahan. Influential classic of naval history and tactics still used as text in war colleges. First paperback edition. 4 maps. 24 battle plans. 640pp. 5⅜ x 8½. 25509-3

THE STORY OF THE TITANIC AS TOLD BY ITS SURVIVORS, Jack Winocour (ed.). What it was really like. Panic, despair, shocking inefficiency, and a little hero-ism. More thrilling than any fictional account. 26 illustrations. 320pp. 5⅜ x 8½.
20610-6

FAIRY AND FOLK TALES OF THE IRISH PEASANTRY, William Butler Yeats (ed.). Treasury of 64 tales from the twilight world of Celtic myth and legend: "The Soul Cages," "The Kildare Pooka," "King O'Toole and his Goose," many more. Introduction and Notes by W. B. Yeats. 352pp. 5⅜ x 8½.
26941-8

BUDDHIST MAHAYANA TEXTS, E. B. Cowell and others (eds.). Superb, accu-rate translations of basic documents in Mahayana Buddhism, highly important in his-tory of religions. The Buddha-karita of Asvaghosha, Larger Sukhavativyuha, more. 448pp. 5⅜ x 8½.
25552-2

ONE TWO THREE . . . INFINITY: Facts and Speculations of Science, George Gamow. Great physicist's fascinating, readable overview of contemporary science: number theory, relativity, fourth dimension, entropy, genes, atomic structure, much more. 128 illustrations. Index. 352pp. 5⅜ x 8½.
25664-2

EXPERIMENTATION AND MEASUREMENT, W. J. Youden. Introductory man-ual explains laws of measurement in simple terms and offers tips for achieving accu-racy and minimizing errors. Mathematics of measurement, use of instruments, exper-imenting with machines. 1994 edition. Foreword. Preface. Introduction. Epilogue. Selected Readings. Glossary. Index. Tables and figures. 128pp. 5⅜ x 8½. 40451-X

DALÍ ON MODERN ART: The Cuckolds of Antiquated Modern Art, Salvador Dalí. Influential painter skewers modern art and its practitioners. Outrageous evaluations of Picasso, Cézanne, Turner, more. 15 renderings of paintings discussed. 44 calligraphic decorations by Dalí. 96pp. 5⅜ x 8½. (Available in U.S. only.)
29220-7

ANTIQUE PLAYING CARDS: A Pictorial History, Henry René D'Allemagne. Over 900 elaborate, decorative images from rare playing cards (14th–20th centuries): Bacchus, death, dancing dogs, hunting scenes, royal coats of arms, players cheating, much more. 96pp. 9¼ x 12¼.
29265-7

MAKING FURNITURE MASTERPIECES: 30 Projects with Measured Drawings, Franklin H. Gottshall. Step-by-step instructions, illustrations for constructing hand-some, useful pieces, among them a Sheraton desk, Chippendale chair, Spanish desk, Queen Anne table and a William and Mary dressing mirror. 224pp. 8⅛ x 11¼.
29338-6

THE FOSSIL BOOK: A Record of Prehistoric Life, Patricia V. Rich et al. Profusely illustrated definitive guide covers everything from single-celled organisms and dinosaurs to birds and mammals and the interplay between climate and man. Over 1,500 illustrations. 760pp. 7½ x 10⅛.
29371-8

Paperbound unless otherwise indicated. Available at your book dealer, online at **www.doverpublications.com**, or by writing to Dept. GI, Dover Publications, Inc., 31 East 2nd Street, Mineola, NY 11501. For current price information or for free catalogues (please indicate field of interest), write to Dover Publications or log on to **www.doverpublications.com** and see every Dover book in print. Dover publishes more than 500 books each year on science, elementary and advanced mathematics, biology, music, art, literary history, social sciences, and other areas.